A Handbook of
Structured
Experiences
for
Human
Relations
Training

Volume X

Edited by

J. WILLIAM PFEIFFER, Ph.D., J.D.

UNIVERSITY ASSOCIATES
Publishers and Consultants
8517 Production Avenue
San Diego, California 92121

SERIES IN HUMAN RESOURCE DEVELOPMENT

Copyright © 1985 by University Associates, Inc.

ISBN: 0-88390-184-6

Library of Congress Catalog Card Number 73-92840

The materials that appear in this book (except those for which reprint permission must be obtained from the primary sources) may be reproduced for educational/ training activities. Special permission for such uses is not required. However, we do ask that the following statement appear on all reproductions:

This permission statement is limited to the reproduction of materials for educational/training events. *Systematic* or *large-scale reproduction* or distribution—or inclusion of items in publications for sale—may be done only with prior written permission.

Printed in the United States of America

PREFACE

The tenth volume of the *Handbook* series has proved to be as interesting a project as its predecessors. Innovative structured experiences continue to be submitted, and I remain impressed with the work being done by group facilitators in this country and abroad.

The twenty-four structured experiences in this volume address a variety of training topics and issues. As in the earlier volumes, most of the twenty-four are new; a few are new variations of training designs that will allow you to incorporate fresh content into some of your favorites. Care has been taken in the selection of all twenty-four to ensure that they offer ways to help participants to increase their understanding of the world in which they live and work.

We at University Associates continue to hold the professional value that resources should be shared by peers. The *Handbooks of Structured Experiences for Human Relations Training* are one important evidence of this belief. We invite users to participate in this process through feedback suggestions. All of the materials in the *Handbooks* may be freely reproduced for educational or training purposes. For large-scale distribution or the inclusion of materials in publications for sale, prior written permission is required.

I would like to express my appreciation to the colleagues who have contributed to this volume and to the expert editorial system that produced it. I particularly wish to thank Beverly Byrum, facilitator and content consultant; Mary Kitzmiller, managing editor; Carol Nolde, senior editor; and Jacqueline Pickett, typographer.

J. William Pfeiffer

San Diego, California
May, 1985

TABLE OF CONTENTS

*See Introduction, p. 3, for explanation of numbering.

INTRODUCTION

Our early work in creating learning designs led us to the use of what had always been termed "exercises," "techniques," or "games." When we made the decision to gather these valuable materials into a book, we became concerned that "exercise" and "game" had connotations we considered dysfunctional to the intent of their use. We therefore elected to call them "structured experiences" to indicate that they are designed for experience-based learning.

Our interest in providing participants with a distinctive design for human relations training has resulted in an increasing orientation in our consulting activities and workshops toward experiences that produce generally predictable outcomes. In designing human relations training experiences, we strive to become aware of and to examine the specific needs of the client system or particular group and then develop learning situations that will meet those needs. Based on an experiential model, structured experiences are inductive rather than deductive, providing *direct* rather than vicarious learnings. Thus, participants *discover* meaning for themselves and *validate* their own experience.

A variety of experiential learning models have been developed in recent years (see Palmer, 1981). Our own version has five steps that occur in a cycle:

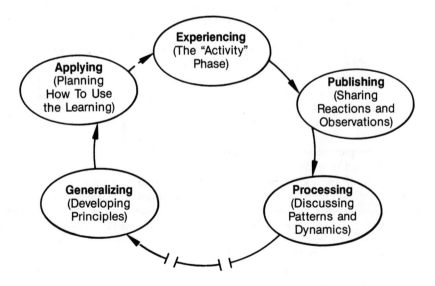

The *experiencing* phase involves some activity such as fantasy, dyadic sharing, or group problem solving. If the model stopped at this point, however, training

1

would be only "fun and games." Next the participants engage in *publishing* their reactions to and observations of the activity. This is the data-generation phase; it leads logically into *processing*. It is our belief that processing is the key to the potency of structured experiences, and it is important that the facilitator allow sufficient time for this step. If the training is to transfer to the "real world," it is important for the participants to be able to extrapolate the experience from a laboratory setting to the outside world through *generalizing*. In this phase participants develop principles, hypotheses, and generalizations that can be discussed in the final phase, *applying*. This final phase must not be left to chance; facilitators need to ensure that participants recognize the relevance of the learning. The actual application of behavior becomes a new experience and begins the cycle again.

There is no successful way to cut short this cycle. If structured experiences are to be effective, the facilitator must supply adequate opportunities for "talk-through." The payoff comes when the participants learn *useful* things that they take responsibility for applying.

Thus, a concern that we bring to all our training publications is the need for adequate processing of the training experience so that participants are able to integrate the learning without the stress generated by unresolved feelings about the experience. It is at this point that the expertise of the facilitator becomes crucial if the experience is to be responsive to the learning and emotional needs of the participants. The facilitator must judge whether he or she will be able successfully to process the data that probably will emerge in the group through the structured experience. Any facilitator, regardless of background, who is committed to the growth of individuals in the group can usefully employ structured experiences.

The choice of a particular activity must be made using two criteria: the facilitator's competence and the participants' needs. It is the responsibility of the facilitator to examine his or her own expertise as well as the specific needs and the level of sophistication of the group involved. Adaptability and flexibility are, therefore, emphasized in the design of the structured experiences in this volume. The variations listed after each structured experience suggest possible alterations that a facilitator may wish to incorporate in order to make the experience more suitable to the particular design and to the needs of the participants. The expected norm in human relations training is innovation.

Our use of and experimentation with structured experiences led us to an interest in developing useful, uncomplicated questionnaires, opinionnaires, and other instruments. It is our belief that instruments enhance and reinforce the learning from structured experiences. Instruments also provide feedback to the facilitator on the appropriateness of the activity and the effectiveness of the presentation.

Some instruments appeared in the first volumes of the *Handbooks* and have subsequently been revised and refined in later editions. Each volume of the *Handbook* contains structured experiences that include instruments. We find that the complementary selection of structured experiences and instruments can create powerful learning environments for participants, and we encourage those involved in the field of human resource development to become acquainted with this two-fold approach in providing for participants' learning needs. In addition, Volume X includes lecturette content whenever a lecturette is part of the design of a structured experience.

At the end of each structured experience in this volume are any appropriate cross-references to similar structured experiences, suggested instruments, and/or lecturette sources. The number of each supplemental or complementary structured experience and the publication in which it appears are indicated. Instruments and lecturettes are listed by title, publication, and page number. Space for notes on each structured experience has been provided for the convenience of the facilitator.

The sequencing of structured experiences in Volume X is different from that of the previous volumes of the *Handbook*. The sequence in Volumes I through IX is based on the amount of understanding, skill, and experience needed by the facilitator to use each experience effectively. In each of those volumes, therefore, the first structured experience requires much less background on the part of the facilitator than does the last. In Volume X the order of structured experiences has been changed to reflect their classification into categories according to their focus and intent. A listing of these categories can be found on page 155 in this book; an explanation of the categorization scheme can be found in the "User's Guide" to *The Structured Experience Kit*, in the section entitled "Classification of Structured Experiences" in the *Reference Guide to Handbooks and Annuals,* and in the "Introduction to the Structured Experiences Section" of the 1981 *Annual.* This category system was developed for *The Structured Experience Kit,* which contains structured experiences from all volumes of the *Handbook* and all volumes of the *Annual.* One feature of the *Kit* is that each experience has been rated according to (a) how much affect is likely to be generated, (b) how structurally complex the design is, and (c) how difficult the activity is to process.

Our published structured experiences are numbered consecutively throughout the series of *Handbooks* and *Annuals,* in order of publication of the volumes. The contents of the entire series of *Handbooks* and *Annuals* are fully indexed in the *Reference Guide to Handbooks and Annuals.* The *Reference Guide* is an indispensable aid in locating a particular structured experience or a structured experience for a particular purpose, as well as related instruments, lecturettes, and theory articles.

The purpose, then, of the *Handbooks* is to share further the training materials that we have found to be useful in training designs. Some of the experiences that appear here originated within University Associates, and some were submitted to us by facilitators in the field. It is gratifying to find that facilitators around the world are using the *Handbooks* and concur with our philosophy that sharing these valuable materials with others is far more in the spirit of human relations theory than the stagnating concept of "ownership" of ideas.

Users are encouraged to submit structured experiences, instruments they have developed, and papers they have written that might be of interest to practitioners in human resource development. In this manner, our Series in Human Resource Development will continue to serve as a clearinghouse for ideas developed by group facilitators.

REFERENCE

Palmer, A. Learning cycles: Models of behavioral change. In J. E. Jones & J. W. Pfeiffer (Eds.), *The 1981 annual handbook for group facilitators.* San Diego, CA: University Associates, 1981.

389. ALOHA: A FEEDBACK EXPERIENCE

Goals

    I. To offer the participants an opportunity to give and receive feedback about their strengths and opportunities for improvement in interpersonal relations.

    II. To provide closure at the end of an experiential-learning event.

Group Size

    Any number of groups of approximately five to eight participants each. (The composition of each group should be the same as that used throughout the experiential-learning event.)

Time Required

    Approximately forty-five minutes.

Materials

    A tennis ball for each group.

Physical Setting

    A room with a movable chair for each participant.

Process

    I. The facilitator begins by saying that Hawaii is nicknamed "the Aloha State" and that many visitors to Hawaii have learned about the spirit of aloha. The participants are told that the word "aloha" means "hello" and "good-by" and implies a wish for hope, love, peace, happiness, and friendship. The facilitator explains that the final group session will be based on the spirit of aloha and the giving and receiving of feedback, all of which are particularly appropriate when an experiential-learning event is being completed and the participants are meeting for the last time.

    II. The participants are asked to assemble into their customary groups, and the members of each group are asked to be seated in a circle. The facilitator explains that he or she will toss a tennis ball to one member of each group in order to start the process. The group member who has received the tennis ball will be the first to receive feedback from each of his or her fellow members. The facilitator stipulates that the feedback is to focus on the recipient's strengths in interpersonal relations as well as areas in interpersonal relations that the recipient might want to consider as opportunities for growth and improvement. The facilitator further explains that the recipient is to listen to all feedback without comment, except when clarification is needed. When all feedback has been given, the recipient is to toss the tennis ball to another member, without announcing beforehand who the new recipient will be. Subsequently, this process is to be repeated until all of the participants have received feedback from all of their fellow group members. After explaining the procedure, the facilitator tosses a tennis ball to one member in each group and asks the participants to begin. (Twenty-five minutes.)

III. When the feedback process has been completed, the facilitator elicits any other comments that the participants would like to make. Then the members of each group are instructed to say "aloha" to one another in any way they wish before leaving the session. The participants are also encouraged to repeat the "aloha" process with members of other groups as well.

Variations

I. Leis may be substituted for the tennis balls. In this case the facilitator places a lei around the neck of one member in each group to begin the feedback process; when all feedback has been given, the recipient removes the lei and places it around the neck of another member, who becomes the next recipient of feedback.

II. In Step III the facilitator may point out that the Hawaiian word "ohana" means a tightly knit, small group and that the participants may want to express to one another what their experiences in their small groups have meant to them throughout the course of the experiential-learning event.

III. In Step III each group member may be given a flower. One member puts his or her flower in the center of the circle and shares a sentiment about the group as a whole. Then the other members take turns completing this process.

Similar Structured Experiences: *'75 Annual:* Structure Experience **146**; *'78 Annual:* **225**; *Vol. IX:* **355**.

Submitted by Thomas H. Patten, Jr.

Notes on the Use of "Aloha":

390. I AM, DON'T YOU THINK?: ZODIAC FEEDBACK

Goals

I. To assist the participants in gaining insight about themselves and about their fellow group members.

II. To provide the participants with an opportunity to compare their self-perceptions with others' perceptions of them.

III. To heighten the participants' awareness of the ways in which a variety of member characteristics can enrich a group.

Group Size

Two or three groups (a maximum of thirty participants). The members of each group should be acquainted with one another.

Time Required

Approximately two hours.

Materials

I. A copy of the I Am, Don't You Think? Characteristics Sheet for each participant.

II. A copy of the I Am, Don't You Think? Zodiac Key for each participant.

III. A copy of the I Am, Don't You Think? Zodiac Signs Handout for each participant.

IV. A copy of the I Am, Don't You Think? Discussion Sheet for each participant.

V. A pencil for each participant.

VI. For each participant, enough 3 " x 5 " index cards to equal the number of other members in that participant's group. (For example, if there are six members in one group, each member of that group receives five 3 " x 5 " cards.)

Physical Setting

A room with chairs and writing surfaces for the participants.

Process

I. The facilitator introduces the goals of the activity and asks the participants to assemble into their groups.

II. Each participant is given a copy of the characteristics sheet and a pencil and is asked to read all forty-eight characteristics listed on this sheet. After the participants have finished reading, the facilitator instructs each participant to work independently to select the *ten* characteristics that describe himself or herself best and to place a check mark in the "My Opinion" column beside each of these ten. (Fifteen minutes.)

III. The facilitator gives each participant the appropriate number of 3 " x 5 " index cards. Each participant is instructed to consider each of the other group members in turn, to write this person's name on one of the 3 " x 5 " cards, to select *four* characteristics from the sheet that best describe this person, and to write the *numbers* of these four characteristics on the card below the person's name. The participants are asked not to consult one another while they complete this task. (Twenty minutes.)

IV. After each participant has completed a card for every other member of his or her group, the facilitator asks the participants to distribute their cards to the people whose names appear on the cards. Then the participants are instructed to go through their cards one by one; each participant is told to refer to the characteristics sheet and to tally the contents of the received cards by placing a tick mark in the "Others' Opinions" column to indicate each time a specific characteristic is noted by number.

V. Each participant is instructed to write the number of matches between the self-assessments and others' assessments in the appropriate places in the "Number of Matches" column, to determine his or her score, to write it in the blank provided, and to determine the consistency between the self-assessments and others' assessments.

VI. The facilitator distributes copies of the zodiac key and asks each participant to compare his or her matches with the characteristics that are representative of his or her sign.

VII. Each participant is given a copy of the zodiac signs handout and is instructed to read the entire list of characteristics for his or her sign. In addition, the facilitator distributes copies of the discussion sheet and asks the members of each group to read and follow the instructions on this sheet and to select one member to lead them in their discussion. (Forty-five minutes.)

Structured Experience   **390**

VIII. The facilitator reassembles the total group and leads a concluding discussion about the ways in which the participants can use what they have learned to improve their interaction with their fellow group members.

Variations

I. The participants may be encouraged to give and receive additional feedback about characteristics they especially like in their fellow group members, characteristics that their fellow members might want to emphasize more, and/or characteristics that they would like to develop for personal growth.

II. The zodiac model may be eliminated, and the participants may be asked simply to complete the characteristics sheet and to provide one another with feedback.

Similar Structured Experiences: *Volume III:* Structured Experience **58**; *'78 Annual:* **225**.
Suggested Instruments: *'80 Annual,* p. 89: "Personal Style Inventory"; *Vol. IX,* p. 61: "Personality Traits Inventory."

Notes on the Use of "I Am, Don't You Think?":

Submitted by Jane C. Bryant.

I AM, DON'T YOU THINK? CHARACTERISTICS SHEET

Characteristic	My Opinion	Others' Opinions	Number of Matches
1. is determined, ambitious			
2. assesses situations quickly			
3. thrives on constant activity			
4. possesses a firm sense of values; is trustworthy			
5. has strong nurturing instincts			
6. has a sense of discipline and purpose			
7. has a progressive outlook			
8. is independent; needs privacy			
9. has an ability to relieve the suffering of others			
10. has a pioneering, adventurous spirit			
11. exhibits considerable interest in health and hygiene			
12. likes to have power and authority			
13. is refined, diplomatic, tactful			
14. is brave, with little regard for danger			
15. is good at coping with life			
16. pursues causes; is often in favor of change			
17. has leadership ability			
18. is idealistic; shows strong sense of justice			
19. has excellent business sense			
20. is a generous, loving, devoted friend			
21. is a nonconformist			

Characteristic	My Opinion	Others' Opinions	Number of Matches
22. is able to see clearly all sides of a situation			
23. is dynamic, fascinating, mysterious			
24. is conventional, rational, serious			
25. is impulsive, spontaneous			
26. enjoys country living, gardening			
27. is a wonderful lover with a flair for the romantic			
28. exhibits a flair for writing and languages			
29. is domestic; loves home			
30. needs a challenge; likes to show initiative			
31. is original, inventive, resourceful			
32. has a tendency to flirt			
33. is easygoing, good-natured			
34. knows a little bit about a lot of things			
35. prizes harmony and pleasant living conditions			
36. loves animals			
37. possesses great personal magnetism			
38. is proud, self-confident			
39. likes "important" work, not trivialities			
40. likes detail; is good at organizing			
41. is passionate in politics, work, play			
42. presents a solid, steady, reliable front to the world			

Characteristic	My Opinion	Others' Opinions	Number of Matches
43. is receptive and devoted to others			
44. is intellectual, logical, busy			
45. exhibits a sense of showmanship and drama			
46. has a humanitarian, reforming, altruistic spirit			
47. likes "doing" and "making" hobbies			
48. has a strong sense of responsibility			

Total Number of Matches Divided by Number of Others' Opinions = Score:

_____ ÷ _____ = _____

Scoring Scale
3.1 - 4.0 = High Consistency
2.1 - 3.0 = Moderate Consistency
1.1 - 2.0 = Moderate Discrepancy
0 - 1.0 = High Discrepancy

I AM, DON'T YOU THINK? ZODIAC KEY

The numbers listed below for each of the twelve zodiac signs correspond to the numbers assigned to the characteristics on the characteristics sheet. Although each of the four characteristics listed for each sign is representative of that sign, you should note that many characteristics are shared by different signs. You should also note that different astrologers may list slightly different dates for the various signs.

Aries (March 21- April 20)	Taurus (April 21- May 21)	Gemini (May 22- June 21)
2	19	28
10	4	32
14	26	34
30	42	44

Cancer (June 22- July 23)	Leo (July 24- August 23)	Virgo (August 24- September 23)
5	12	3
20	17	11
29	38	40
48	45	47

Libra (September 24- October 23)	Scorpio (October 24- November 22)	Sagittarius (November 23- December 21)
13	23	8
18	37	21
22	39	25
35	41	36

Capricorn (December 22- January 20)	Aquarius (January 21- February 19)	Pisces (February 20- March 20)
1	7	9
6	16	27
15	31	33
24	46	43

I AM, DON'T YOU THINK? ZODIAC SIGNS HANDOUT

Aries (March 21-April 20)

1. assesses situations quickly
2. has a pioneering, adventurous spirit
3. is vigorous, enthusiastic, highly energetic
4. hates restrictions; loves freedom
5. is self-sufficient, independent, self-assured
6. is honest and direct with others
7. is inquisitive
8. loves competitive work
9. needs a challenge; likes to show initiative
10. participates in/enjoys vigorous sports
11. is intelligent, capable, dynamic
12. likes a busy, active life style
13. is brave, with little regard for danger
14. is enterprising, ambitious; works hard

Taurus (April 21-May 21)

1. is practical, conservative, cautious
2. is reliable, patient, enduring
3. loves luxury and good food
4. is persistent, strong willed
5. is affectionate, warm hearted, friendly
6. possesses a firm sense of values; is trustworthy
7. presents a solid, steady, reliable front to the world
8. needs security in career, home, marriage
9. has a well-developed sense of self-preservation
10. has excellent business sense
11. enjoys country living, gardening
12. needs a conventional office life and a guaranteed paycheck
13. enjoys music and art
14. is good at team sports

These characteristics have been adapted from several different sources.

Structured Experience 390

Gemini (May 22-June 21)

1. is adaptable, versatile
2. is intellectual, logical, busy
3. is witty, lively, talkative
4. knows a little bit about a lot of things
5. can "bluff out of tight corners"
6. needs variety and change
7. is capricious, inquisitive
8. has a penchant for media and communications work
9. has a tendency to flirt
10. likes all kinds of people
11. exhibits a flair for writing and languages
12. demonstrates a considerable talent for conversing
13. is eager to express opinions
14. is energetic; needs mental stimulation

Cancer (June 22-July 23)

1. has strong nurturing instincts
2. is solicitous, protective
3. is cautious, shrewd
4. is kind, sensitive, sympathetic
5. is sentimental, romantic
6. is domestic; loves home
7. cherishes marriage
8. has imaginative powers and a good memory
9. has an extremely organized mind
10. needs a calm working atmosphere
11. has a strong sense of responsibility
12. is emotionally resourceful
13. is helpful, thoughtful, understanding
14. is a generous, loving, devoted friend

Leo (July 24-August 23)

1. is magnanimous
2. is proud, self-confident
3. is broad-minded, expansive
4. exhibits a sense of showmanship and drama
5. has leadership ability
6. possesses natural, spontaneous charm
7. is affectionate, cheerful, optimistic
8. is extravagant
9. works hard; sets a good example for others
10. likes to have power and authority
11. is a constructive, quick thinker
12. is loyal and expressive in love
13. demonstrates natural exuberance and enthusiasm
14. is an excellent, motivating teacher

Virgo (August 24-September 23)

1. is discriminating, analytical, practical
2. is tidy, neat, fastidious
3. works hard
4. is careful, cautious
5. thrives on constant activity
6. strives for perfection
7. enjoys learning
8. exhibits considerable interest in health and hygiene
9. likes detail; is good at organizing
10. is a good follower who lends stability and practical help
11. is modest
12. is kind, caring
13. needs financial security
14. likes "doing" and "making" hobbies

Libra (September 24-October 23)

1. has a romantic nature
2. is idealistic; shows strong sense of justice
3. is refined, diplomatic, tactful
4. prizes harmony and pleasant living conditions
5. likes to socialize
6. loves the good life
7. possesses natural charm with a winning manner
8. is an excellent, thoughtful entertainer
9. is able to see clearly all sides of a situation
10. is warm, kind, affectionate
11. is witty, clever
12. is anxious to love and to share life experiences
13. is creative, appreciative of art
14. is fun to be with

Scorpio (October 24-November 22)

1. is a loyal friend and mate
2. feels a strong sense of purpose
3. is highly imaginative, discerning, subtle
4. is persistent, determined
5. is passionate in politics, work, play
6. is courageous, self-sufficient
7. is kind and compassionate
8. possesses great personal magnetism
9. is dynamic, fascinating, mysterious
10. is intuitive, perceptive, insightful
11. loves intensely, ardently, enduringly
12. likes to tax abilities to fullest extent
13. has a philosophical nature
14. likes "important" work, not trivialities

Sagittarius (November 23-December 21)

1. is jovial, cheerful, optimistic
2. loves life
3. is sincere, frank
4. is scrupulous, idealistic
5. has a wide variety of interests
6. is impulsive, spontaneous
7. is a nonconformist
8. is independent; needs privacy
9. is active, energetic
10. needs physical and intellectual exercise
11. enjoys challenges and exploration of the unknown
12. loves animals
13. likes to have a large circle of acquaintances
14. is benevolent, kind

Capricorn (December 22-January 20)

1. is driven to achieve
2. is loyal, sincere, supportive
3. likes to take charge, to be in control
4. is determined, ambitious
5. values family life
6. is concerned with career and prestige
7. has a sense of discipline and purpose
8. is patient, persevering
9. exhibits a cool and calculating mental outlook
10. is shy but cherishing and protective in love
11. needs job security and regular paychecks
12. likes fame and being in the public eye
13. is conventional, rational, serious
14. is good at coping with life

Aquarius (January 21-February 19)

1. has a humanitarian, reforming, altruistic spirit
2. is friendly, sincere, loyal
3. has a progressive outlook
4. is original, inventive, resourceful
5. needs personal independence
6. pursues causes; is often in favor of change
7. exhibits an aloof glamour that is compelling
8. is drawn to scientific pursuits
9. approaches problems analytically
10. is intelligent, inquisitive, observant
11. is a good listener
12. loves mental challenges
13. is idealistic; prizes truth
14. looks at the world in new ways

Pisces (February 20-March 20)

1. is kind, compassionate, sympathetic
2. is impressionable
3. is sensitive, intuitive, meditative
4. seeks contentment more than achievement
5. is receptive and devoted to others
6. is a wonderful lover with a flair for the romantic
7. needs to be loved and needed
8. has an ability to relieve the suffering of others
9. appreciates, enjoys, and is inspired by the arts
10. is flexible in dealing with people
11. needs a congenial environment at home and at work
12. is easygoing, good-natured
13. is patient, self-sacrificing
14. is easily carried away in emotional relationships

I AM, DON'T YOU THINK? DISCUSSION SHEET

Instructions: You and your fellow group members are to discuss answers to the following questions. During this discussion you should state your own answer to each question and encourage your fellow members to do the same. The more fully you participate, the more you will learn about yourself and the other members.

1. What was your consistency score? How do you feel about this score?
2. Which characteristics from your zodiac sheet do you feel are most descriptive of you?
3. How accurate do you feel your self-assessment was? How accurate were your fellow group members' assessments of you?
4. How did you feel about assessing yourself? How did you feel about assessing the other members? How did you feel about having others assess you?
5. What similarities did you discover among yourselves? What differences did you find?
6. How do these similarities and differences enrich your group? How do the similarities contribute to group cohesiveness? How do the differences contribute to group vitality? How do similarities and differences work together to make a fully functioning group?
7. What did you learn about yourself that you had not realized before?
8. What did you learn about your fellow group members?

391. TWO BAGS FULL: FEEDBACK ABOUT MANAGERIAL CHARACTERISTICS

Goals

 I. To offer the participants an opportunity to provide one another with feedback about their managerial traits and behaviors.

 II. To help each participant to determine his or her strengths and avenues for growth as a manager.

 III. To assist each participant in developing a set of action steps for personal growth as a manager.

Group Size

All members of an intact managerial group; a group with more than eight members should be accommodated in two sessions. It is advisable for the participants to have had some previous team-building experience.

Time Required

Two hours.

Materials

 I. For each participant, a number of 3″ x 5″ cards equivalent to twice the number of members in the group minus two. For example, if the group consists of six members, each participant receives ten 3″ x 5″ cards.

 II. A pencil for each participant.

 III. A portable writing surface for each participant.

 IV. Two small paper bags for each participant.

 V. A newsprint flip chart and a felt-tipped marker.

Physical Setting

Any room in which the group normally meets.

Process

I. The facilitator begins the activity by stating that one way to perceive the role of a manager is to see him or her as a person who fulfills four kinds of expectations:

1. Expectations of subordinates, which include receiving feedback about performance;

2. Expectations of peers, which include being kept informed about the manager's activities;

3. Expectations of the manager's supervisor, which include implementing the organization's policies; and

4. Self-expectations, which include attending to the manager's own professional development.

II. The facilitator guides the participants through a fantasy experience by making the following comments, pausing briefly after each.

1. Think about the best manager you have ever had or known.

2. Close your eyes, relax, and visualize this person.

3. What did this person expect of you?

4. What did this person expect of your co-workers?

5. How did this person behave toward subordinates?

6. How did this person behave toward his or her peers?

7. How did this person behave toward his or her supervisor?

8. What particular things did this person say and do that made him or her a top-notch manager?

9. What standards did this person set for himself or herself?

10. When you have this person clearly in mind, feel free to open your eyes.

III. The participants are asked to volunteer traits and behaviors that were characteristic of the managers they visualized. As these traits and behaviors are mentioned, the facilitator records them on newsprint. (Ten minutes.)

IV. The facilitator distributes 3 " x 5 " cards, pencils, portable writing surfaces, and paper bags. Each participant is instructed to write the word "strengths" on one of his or her paper bags and the words "avenues for growth" on the other.

V. The facilitator explains that each participant is to consider the managerial attributes of every other participant in turn: The participant is to consult the newsprint list, to choose one of the traits or behaviors listed that is a *strength* for the other participant under consideration, and to write this trait or behavior anonymously on a 3 " x 5 " card; then he or she is to choose a trait or behavior that represents an *avenue for growth* for the other participant and to write this trait or behavior anonymously on a separate 3 " x 5 " card. Subsequently, he or she is to deposit the 3 " x 5 " cards in the appropriate paper bags belonging to the other participant. This procedure is to be followed until each participant has deposited two cards in the appropriate bags for every other participant. After answering any questions about the procedure, the facilitator instructs the participants to begin. (Fifteen minutes.)

VI. Each participant in turn shares his or her designated *strengths* with the rest of the group by reading aloud the 3 " x 5 " cards that have been deposited in the paper bag labeled "strengths." After reading all of his or her cards, the participant asks any questions necessary for clarification and states any reactions to the feedback presented. During this phase of the activity, none of the remaining participants identify their own comments unless they choose to do so. (Twenty minutes.)

VII. The facilitator instructs each participant to read privately the contents of his or her paper bag labeled "avenues for growth" and to select one such avenue that he or she is interested in pursuing and is willing to share with the group. Then each participant in turn reads aloud the chosen 3 " x 5 " card and receives feedback from the remaining participants regarding this behavior and how this avenue of growth might be pursued. As part of this process, the participant receiving feedback also contracts with his or her fellow participants to take specific action steps in pursuit of the chosen avenue of growth and writes these steps on the back of his or her 3 " x 5 " card. In addition, arrangements are made for a follow-up meeting to determine progress and any further action steps to be taken. (Forty-five minutes.)

VIII. The facilitator leads a concluding discussion by asking the following questions:

1. What was your reaction to reviewing your strengths as others saw them? What was your reaction to reviewing your avenues for growth?

2. What patterns did you find in the feedback you received? What area of emphasis seems to be of most importance: self-development, relationships with your peers, relationships with your subordinates, or your relationship with your supervisor?

3. How do the patterns of your feedback compare with what you know about managing people?

4. What are some of the action steps that you have decided to take before the follow-up meeting?

5. What other contracts do you need to make to ensure your progress?

Variations

I. A communication instrument may be administered before the feedback is given so that each manager can discover patterns that are common to his or her self-report and the peer feedback.

II. In Step V each manager may be asked to predict what he or she thinks others will identify as strengths and avenues for growth.

III. After Step VII the facilitator may deliver a lecturette on theory and research about effective managerial behaviors.

IV. Specific strengths and avenues for growth may serve as the focus of separate sessions. For example, sessions may be conducted on self-development, relationships with peers, relationships with subordinates, or relationships with supervisors.

Similar Structured Experiences: *'78 Annual:* Structured Experience 225.
Suggested Instruments: *Volume I,* p. 10: "T-P Leadership Questionnaire"; *'72 Annual,* p. 65: "Supervisory Attitudes: The X-Y Scale"; *'76 Annual,* p. 89: "Leader Effectiveness and Adaptability Description (LEAD)"; *'82 Annual,* p. 110: "Managerial Attitude Questionnaire"; *'83 Annual,* p. 22: "Manager's Dilemma Work Sheet."

Notes on the Use of "Two Bags Full":

Submitted by Alan R. Carey.

392. WATER JARS: DEVELOPING CREATIVITY IN PROBLEM SOLVING

Goals

    I. To demonstrate the development of mental blocks in problem solving.

    II. To illustrate that the process of solving problems of a repetitive nature poses a threat to creativity.

    III. To allow the participants to investigate ways of breaking mental blocks and fostering creative problem solving.

Group Size

    Any number of participants.

Time Required

    Approximately forty-five minutes.

Materials

    I. A copy of the Water Jars Work Sheet for each participant.

    II. A pencil for each participant.

    III. A newsprint flip chart and a felt-tipped marker.

Physical Setting

    A room with a chair and a writing surface for each participant.

Process

    I. The facilitator introduces the activity by stating that it involves creative problem solving.

    II. Each participant is given a copy of the Water Jars Work Sheet and a pencil and is asked to read the instructions on the handout. (Five minutes.)

    III. The facilitator clarifies the task involved, emphasizing the rules listed on the work sheet. If asked any questions about the process necessary to arrive at solutions, the facilitator responds, "You have all the information you need in order to complete the task, and you are free to do whatever you like within the rules." (Five minutes.)

IV. The participants are instructed to begin the task. As they work, the facilitator monitors their activity, ensuring that they are attempting the problems one after another in the proper order.

V. After ten minutes the facilitator interrupts the participants, advising them to look at each problem from a different viewpoint and to try new approaches to finding solutions. Then the participants are instructed to continue their work and are reminded not to consult with one another.

VI. If any participants are still working after five more minutes, the facilitator asks them to complete the task quickly so that the group can proceed with the next phase of the activity. Those who are struggling with individual problems are advised to write "no solution" in the space reserved for answers.

VII. The facilitator writes the following formulas on newsprint, announcing that each is one possible solution.

1. $B - A - 2C$ 8. $A + C$
2. $B - A - 2C$ 9. $A - C$
3. $B - A - 2C$ 10. $A + C$
4. $B - A - 2C$ 11. C
5. $B - A - 2C$ 12. $A - C$
6. $B - A - 2C$ 13. $A - C$
7. $A - C$

VIII. The facilitator leads a concluding discussion by asking the following questions:

1. What approach did you take in beginning the task? How did you choose that approach? How did it help or hinder you?
2. What patterns emerged in the sequence of solutions? Who found different solutions and patterns? What were they? How did you come up with them?
3. How did your first few solutions affect your approach to completing the task?
4. How were you affected by the instruction to finish the task in the shortest possible time? How were you affected by the instruction to try new approaches? What did you try? How did your new approaches work?
5. What pitfalls are involved in attempts to solve routine or repetitive problems?

6. How might you guard against these pitfalls?
7. If you were to complete this task again, what would you do differently?
8. How might you foster a creative approach toward solving problems?

Variations

I. After Step VIII the participants may be asked to complete another work sheet similar to the first one so that they can experiment with what they have learned.

II. The work sheet may be amended to include rules that encourage creativity.

Lecturette Source: *'81 Annual:* "Creativity and Creative Problem Solving."

Notes on the Use of "Water Jars":

_____

Submitted by S. Chintamani.

WATER JARS WORK SHEET

The Task

Each of the following problems involves Jars A, B, and C, which contain different quantities of water. For each problem, your task is to use the information provided to determine a formula for arriving at the required amount of water and to write this formula in the space provided in the "Solution" column.

Example: Using the information provided below, determine a formula for the required amount of water.

Amount of Water in Jars (Ounces)			Required Amount of Water (Ounces)
A	*B*	*C*	
6	35	8	13

In this case a possible formula for the solution is B – A – 2C. This formula can be checked as follows: 35 – 6 – (2 × 8) = 13.

Rules

1. Although there is no time limit for the task, you are expected to complete it in the shortest possible time.
2. You must work on the problems in the order in which they are presented.
3. Once you have begun the task, you may not seek clarification from the facilitator.
4. Consultation or discussion with other participants is prohibited.

Problem No.	Amount of Water in Jars (Ounces)			Required Amount of Water (Ounces)	Solution
	A	*B*	*C*		
1.	5	30	2	21	_____
2.	20	130	3	104	_____
3.	14	164	24	102	_____
4.	18	43	10	5	_____
5.	9	44	6	23	_____

Problem No.	Amount of Water in Jars (Ounces)			Required Amount of Water (Ounces)	Solution
	A	B	C		
6.	20	60	6	28	_____
7.	23	49	3	20	_____
8.	15	39	3	18	_____
9.	28	59	3	25	_____
10.	18	48	4	22	_____
11.	29	38	3	3	_____
12.	14	36	8	6	_____
13.	29	76	5	24	_____

393. WORK-NEEDS ASSESSMENT: ACHIEVEMENT, AFFILIATION, AND POWER

Goals

I. To develop the participants' awareness of the individual needs that motivate people to behave in certain ways in the work place.

II. To assist each participant in determining the needs that motivate him or her in the work place.

Group Size

Four to seven groups of four or five participants each.

Time Required

One and one-half hours.

Materials

I. A copy of the Work-Needs Assessment Inventory for each participant.

II. A copy of the Work-Needs Assessment Scoring Sheet for each participant.

III. A copy of the Work-Needs Assessment Theory Sheet for each participant.

IV. A pencil for each participant.

Physical Setting

A room large enough so that the individual groups can work without disturbing one another. A writing surface and a chair should be provided for each participant.

Process

I. The goals of the activity are explained to the participants.

II. Each participant is given a copy of the Work-Needs Assessment Inventory and a pencil and is instructed to complete the inventory. (Fifteen minutes.)

III. Each participant is given a copy of the Work-Needs Assessment Scoring Sheet and is asked to complete the sheet to determine his or her score. The facilitator emphasizes that the scoring process is not intended to assign any participant to a particular category, but rather to provide each participant with information about himself or herself and to gather data for the discussion that will follow. (Ten minutes.)

IV. The facilitator distributes copies of the Work-Needs Assessment Theory Sheet and instructs each participant to read the sheet. After all participants have completed their reading, the facilitator elicits and answers questions about the content of the sheet, clarifying concepts as necessary. (Fifteen minutes.)

V. The participants are assembled into groups of four or five each. The facilitator explains that within each group the members are to share and discuss their scores, their reactions to their scores, and the implications of these scores. (Thirty minutes.)

VI. The facilitator leads a discussion about ways in which the participants may apply what they have learned to their future experiences in the work place. The following questions are asked:

1. What were the highest-priority needs in your group?

2. What does your highest-priority need suggest about the way in which your organization operates?

3. How do your needs fit with those that govern your organization?

4. What generalizations might you make about types of needs and organizational culture?

5. What are some ways in which you could satisfy your needs more effectively?

6. In what ways might you want to adjust the level of your needs? What might you accomplish by doing this? What is a first step that you might take?

Variations

I. After Step V the participants may be asked to return to their groups and to discuss how they would like to change their needs profiles and/or how they can more effectively meet their present needs.

II. The inventory may be adapted to reflect the positions and/or the nature of work in which the participants are involved.

III. The theory sheet may be distributed and discussed before the inventories are completed, and the participants may be asked to predict what their highest-priority needs will be.

Suggested Instruments: *'76 Annual,* p. 101: "Organization Behavior Describer Survey"; *Vol. VIII,* p. 13: "People on the Job Work Sheet"; *'84 Annual,* p. 131: "Quality of Work Life-Conditions/Feelings (QWL-C/F)"; *'85 Annual,* p. 107: "The Personal Value Statement (PVS): An Experiential Learning Instrument," p. 129: "The Entrepreneurial Orientation Inventory: Measuring the Locus of Control."

Lecturette Sources: *'72 Annual,* p. 125: "The Maslow Need Hierarchy," p. 127: "Job Enrichment"; *'75 Annual,* p. 123: "Human Needs and Behavior"; *'76 Annual,* p. 139: "Power"; *'80 Annual,* p. 152: "Job-Related Adaptive Skills: Toward Personal Growth."

Notes on the Use of "Work-Needs Assessment":

Submitted by Patrick Doyle.

WORK-NEEDS ASSESSMENT INVENTORY

Instructions: Each of the following numbered items consists of three statements. For each separate item, rank each of the three statements according to how descriptive it is of *your own* feelings or opinions about work or of your behavior in a work environment. In the blanks provided to the right of the statements, write *1* for the statement that is *most* descriptive, *2* for the statement that is *next most descriptive,* and *3* for the statement that is *least descriptive.*

Some of the statements imply that you are presently a supervisor; if you are not a supervisor, evaluate these statements according to the way in which you believe you would feel, think, or behave if you were.

Rank

1. a. When solving a problem, I like to work by myself and be solely responsible for the solution. _____

   b. When solving a problem, I like to work as part of a team and find a team solution. _____

   c. When solving a problem, I like to work as part of a team, but only if I am in charge. _____

2. a. Managers should set challenging goals for their subordinates. _____

   b. Goals should be set through mutual agreement of team members. _____

   c. It is important to set goals that are within the average individual's capacity to achieve. _____

3. a. My co-workers would describe me as a good listener. _____

   b. People describe me as fluent. _____

   c. I tend to focus my conversations at work on job-related matters. _____

4. a. I enjoy discussions that are directed toward problem solving. _____

   b. I sometimes take an opposing point of view in a discussion just as a matter of interest. _____

   c. I enjoy discussions that enable me to know my fellow workers better. _____

Rank

5. a. I enjoy being perceived as a team member.   _____

   b. Belonging to a specific team is not a priority with me.   _____

   c. I enjoy my individuality; being seen as a team member does not interest me.   _____

6. a. I like to have feedback about how well I have worked with others as a team member.   _____

   b. I like to have specific feedback about how well I have done a job.   _____

   c. I am the best judge of how well I have done a job; raises and/or promotions are the feedback that is important to me.   _____

7. a. The most important aspect of performance analysis is the setting of future goals for an employee.   _____

   b. The most important aspect of performance analysis is the planning of an employee's future development.   _____

   c. The purpose of performance analysis is to isolate what an employee has done correctly and what mistakes he or she has made.   _____

8. a. Conflict is a tool that can be used to arrive at the best possible solution to a problem.   _____

   b. Conflict can be very healthy; it keeps people on their toes.   _____

   c. Conflict should be controlled; teams whose members argue among themselves are seldom productive.   _____

9. a. A factor of concern with any problem solution is its acceptability to the team that must implement it.   _____

   b. If I am convinced that a problem solution will work, I expect it to be implemented and I accept responsibility for the consequences.   _____

   c. If I find a problem solution that works, I want to implement it; prolonging discussion about it with team members is usually a waste of time.   _____

Rank

10. a. If one of my subordinates does something incorrectly, I show him or her how to correct it.   _____

    b. If one of my subordinates does something incorrectly, I discuss the situation with him or her, and we agree to correct it.   _____

    c. If one of my subordinates does something incorrectly, I tell him or her to correct it.   _____

11. a. People should use mistakes as learning tools and thus improve themselves.   _____

    b. I make mistakes, but as long as I am right most of the time, I deserve my job.   _____

    c. I do not like being wrong; I do not make the same mistake twice.   _____

12. a. With hard work and the support of the right management, an individual can overcome most problems.   _____

    b. Hard work can overcome most problems.   _____

    c. A strong commitment can overcome most problems.   _____

13. a. I focus more on my personal relationships with my peers and my supervisor than I do on my relationships with my subordinates.   _____

    b. I spend time and effort developing and improving my personal relationships at work.   _____

    c. I develop personal relationships at work only when they help me to complete my work tasks.   _____

14. a. "Do not step on people on the way up; you may meet them on the way down."   _____

    b. "Nothing succeeds like success."   _____

    c. "Nobody remembers the name of the person who came in second in a race."   _____

Rank

15. a. If I am right, I will win in the long run.   ———

    b. If I am strong in my convictions, I will win in the long run.   ———

    c. I try to be patient with people; doing so pays off in the long run.   ———

16. a. Workers produce satisfactorily when their supervisors work alongside them.   ———

    b. Workers' productivity increases when they have input regarding their job tasks.   ———

    c. Workers must be challenged to reach new heights of excellence.   ———

17. a. I enjoy convincing my fellow team members to do things my way.   ———

    b. As long as a decision is right, whether it was an individual decision or a team decision is not important.   ———

    c. For any decision to become final, all members of the team that will implement it should find it acceptable.   ———

18. a. I work well when I have a personal relationship with my supervisor.   ———

    b. I work well in situations in which I am my own boss.   ———

    c. I work well when I have deadlines to meet.   ———

WORK-NEEDS ASSESSMENT SCORING SHEET

Instructions: Transfer your rankings from the inventory to this sheet. Then add the numbers in each vertical column and write the total in the blank provided. The column with the lowest total represents your first-priority need; the column with the next-lower total represents your second-priority need; and the column with the highest total represents your third-priority need.

Achievement Need	Affiliation Need	Power Need
1a _____	1b _____	1c _____
2c _____	2b _____	2a _____
3c _____	3a _____	3b _____
4a _____	4c _____	4b _____
5b _____	5a _____	5c _____
6b _____	6a _____	6c _____
7a _____	7b _____	7c _____
8a _____	8c _____	8b _____
9c _____	9a _____	9b _____
10a _____	10b _____	10c _____
11b _____	11a _____	11c _____
12b _____	12c _____	12a _____
13c _____	13b _____	13a _____
14b _____	14a _____	14c _____
15a _____	15c _____	15b _____
16a _____	16b _____	16c _____
17b _____	17c _____	17a _____
18c _____	18a _____	18b _____
Total _____	*Total* _____	*Total* _____

WORK-NEEDS ASSESSMENT THEORY SHEET

The McClelland Model

McClelland (1976), the leading researcher on self-concept, has studied human behavior for many years and has theorized that people are motivated by three basic needs: *achievement, affiliation,* and *power.* He has further asserted that although all of us possess all three needs, we possess them in varying degrees; one person's highest-priority need may be achievement, whereas another person's may be affiliation or power. The following paragraphs present a brief description of each need and the ways in which a high degree of each translates into behavior in an organizational setting.

Achievement

People with a high need for achievement enjoy challenging work, but they also want to ensure that they will succeed; tasks that present so great a risk that success is improbable do not interest or motivate them. Consequently, they tend to set conservative goals.

Achievers plan ahead to avoid any serious problems in their undertakings, but the planning function itself is not a source of motivation for them. They enjoy tasks for which they are personally responsible for the outcomes and with which they can be closely associated with the resulting success. They are quite concerned with meeting appropriate deadlines and experience great anxiety about any project until it has been completed successfully. In addition, they require frequent reinforcement consisting of "hard" data such as sales figures, standards, and so forth.

Affiliation

People with a high need for affiliation direct their energies toward the establishment and maintenance of effective working relationships with others. It is the need for affiliation that prompts people to examine the "human" side of decisions that are made within organizations. When this need supersedes that for achievement or power, the concern for receiving approval from and being liked by peers, supervisors, and subordinates becomes a critical factor in decision making and implementation. Whereas achievers focus on deadlines and the objective aspects of decisions, people whose highest-priority need is affiliation focus on the interrelationships that exist among those who are to be affected by the implementation of decisions. As group members, they try to maintain harmony and mutual respect among members while the group undertakes its function or objective.

Adapted from D.C. McClelland, *The Achieving Society,* Irvington, 1976. Used with the permission of the publisher.

Power

"Power" in terms of McClelland's model can be seen as the ability to overcome resistance in achieving an objective or goal (Pfeffer, 1981). People with a high need for power are usually quite fluent; because they enjoy arguing and confronting conflict, speaking skills are important to them. In an organizational setting, they tend to prefer autocratic decision making ("I make the decision, you implement it"), and they tend to see situations as win/lose ("I win, you lose").

Those whose highest-priority need is power are frequently political realists who evaluate situations in light of their political implications and determine a course of action on the basis of the outcome of their evaluations. When combined with a low need for affiliation, a high need for power may lead an individual to consider people as means to an end, and the value of establishing and maintaining satisfactory relationships in the organization may be lost.

REFERENCES

McClelland, D.C. *The achieving society.* New York: Irvington, 1976.

Pfeffer, J. *Power in organizations.* Marshfield, MA: Pitman, 1981.

394. THE EGO-RADIUS MODEL: EVALUATING AND PLANNING LIFE SITUATIONS

Goals

I. To assist each participant in clarifying and evaluating his or her present life situation and in planning the life situation desired in the future.

II. To allow the participants to share their life situations with one another and to experience peer feedback as a part of the life-planning process.

Group Size

Any number of triads.

Time Required

Two hours.

Materials

I. Several sheets of blank paper and a pencil for each participant.

II. A newsprint flip chart and a felt-tipped marker.

Physical Setting

A room in which the triads can work without disturbing one another. Movable chairs and writing surfaces should be provided for the participants.

Process

I. The facilitator introduces the goals, states that the activity is based on Boshear's "Ego-Radius Model," and explains the model as follows:[1]

"Boshear's 'Ego-Radius Model' provides us with a way to clarify and evaluate the relationships, institutions, and concepts that are important in our lives. Once we have clarified and evaluated these factors, we can better plan our life goals in terms of the importance that we want these factors to hold for us in the future.

---

[1]Adapted from W.C. Boshear and K.G. Albrecht, "Ego-Radius," in *Understanding People: Models and Concepts,* University Associates, 1977.

"Boshear suggests that a person who wants to use this model for life evaluation and planning should begin by drawing a circle on a sheet of paper to represent himself or herself. The word 'Self' is written inside this circle. Then the individual determines which factors are important in his or her life at the moment. These factors may include such things as family, job, money, health, friends, home, recognition, religion, country, and/or any others that are appropriate. A circle is drawn to represent each of these factors, and these circles are placed around the 'Self' circle in such a way that relationships among the factors and the self are indicated. For example, if the individual is intensely committed to his or her family, the circle representing family is drawn very close to the 'Self' circle. However, if recognition is a less-important factor in the individual's life at the moment, the circle representing this factor is drawn farther from the 'Self' circle. Relationships among various factors are indicated by clustering them within the same area, and factors that are in conflict are placed on opposite sides and far apart. As each circle representing a factor is drawn, that circle is labeled as to what it represents."

As this use of the model is explained, the facilitator draws an example on newsprint, using his or her own life situation as the basis for the drawing and explaining the resulting configuration of circles. A sample is illustrated below.

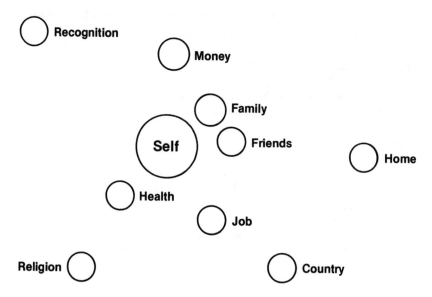

II. Each participant is given several sheets of blank paper and a pencil and is instructed to draw his or her own ego-radius model representing the present life situation. The facilitator remains available during this process to answer questions and to provide assistance as necessary. (Ten minutes.)

III. The facilitator instructs each participant to label the drawing just completed with the words "Present Situation." Then each participant is asked to draw another ego-radius model, this time illustrating the ideal situation that he or she would like to be experiencing in five years. The facilitator stipulates that additional factors should be considered and added where appropriate and that existing factors should be reassessed and adjusted or deleted as necessary. (Ten minutes.)

IV. The facilitator instructs each participant to label the drawing completed in Step III with the words "Ideal Situation in Five Years." Each participant is then asked to draw still another ego-radius model, this time illustrating the situation that is likely to exist in five years if he or she does nothing to achieve the ideal. Again, the facilitator stipulates that factors should be altered, added, and/or deleted as necessary. (Ten minutes.)

V. Each participant is instructed to label the drawing completed in Step IV with the words "Situation in Five Years If No Action Is Taken." Then the participants are asked to assemble into triads and to take turns sharing their three drawings with one another. The facilitator explains that the triad member whose turn it is at the moment is to show and explain each separate plan to the other two members. The other two members are to listen carefully; to ask any questions necessary to understand the drawings; and to help the member who is sharing to clarify relationships, values, and goals and to identify the steps required to realize the ideal situation. The member who is sharing is to take notes during the triad discussion for his or her own personal use. After answering any questions about this procedure, the facilitator instructs the triads to begin. (Fifty minutes.)

VI. After the triads have completed their work, the facilitator reassembles the total group for a discussion of the activity. The following questions are asked:

1. What thoughts and feelings did you experience while drawing your present situation? your ideal situation in five years? your situation in five years if no action is taken?

2. What were the similarities in drawings in your triad? What were the differences? How did each affect you? What did the ego-radius experience symbolize for you?
3. What did your experience teach you about evaluating your life situation and planning for the future? What can you generalize about life planning?
4. What are some steps that you are going to take to realize your ideal situation in five years? How are you going to support yourself in taking those steps?

(Twenty minutes.)

VII. The facilitator encourages each participant to keep his or her drawings and notes, to review them from time to time, to redo any or all of the three drawings as necessary, and to alter as appropriate the steps required to achieve the ideal situation.

Variations

I. In Step III the time frame may be changed to either fewer or more years than five (for example, one year or ten years).

II. After Step VI the participants may be asked to return to their triads to develop written action plans for realizing their ideal situations in five years.

III. Each participant may be asked to draw an ego-radius model illustrating the present situation of the most influential person in his or her life. Subsequently, similarities and differences between each participant's own present situation and that of the influential person are discussed.

Similar Structured Experiences: *Vol. II:* Structured Experience **46**; *'85 Annual:* **378**.
Suggested Instrument: *'85 Annual,* p. 18: "Life Assessment and Planning Guide."

Based on W.C. Boshear and K.G. Albrecht, "Ego-Radius," in *Understanding People: Models and Concepts,* University Associates, 1977.

Notes on the Use of "The Ego-Radius Model":

395. I'M ALL EARS: ENHANCING AWARENESS OF EFFECTIVE LISTENING

Goals

 I. To develop the participants' awareness of some of the requirements for listening effectively.

 II. To explore the effects of distractions on a person's ability to listen.

Group Size

   Two to four groups of six to eight participants each.

Time Required

   One hour and forty-five minutes.

Materials

 I. A copy of the I'm All Ears Reading Sheet for each reader and each observer.

 II. A copy of the I'm All Ears Observer Sheet for each observer.

 III. A copy of the I'm All Ears Retention Test for each listener.

 IV. A copy of the I'm All Ears Scoring Sheet for each listener.

 V. A pencil for each observer and each listener.

Physical Setting

   A large room in which each group can complete its listening task without disturbing the other group(s). The facilitator should plan the arrangement of the room carefully so that each group is allowed as much privacy as possible. A table and chairs should be provided for each group, and a separate table and chairs should be provided for each reader-observer dyad (see Step VII).
   A separate room should be provided for the purpose of preparing the readers and observers for their tasks.

Process

I. The facilitator announces that the activity concentrates on listening and reviews the following deterrents to effective listening:[1]

1. Assuming in advance that the subject is uninteresting and unimportant;
2. Mentally criticizing the speaker's delivery;
3. Becoming overstimulated when questioning or opposing an idea;
4. Listening only for facts, wanting to skip the details;
5. Pretending to be attentive;
6. Allowing the speaker to be inaudible;
7. Avoiding messages whose content is technical;
8. Overreacting to certain words and phrases; and
9. Withdrawing attention and daydreaming.

Questions about these deterrents are elicited and answered. (Fifteen minutes.)

II. Groups of six to eight participants each are assembled and are seated at separate tables. The participants are told that during the activity the members of each group will be given an opportunity to practice effective listening while a fellow member reads a particular piece of copy to them. Each group is asked to select one member to be that group's reader and one member to be the observer.

III. The readers and observers are asked to leave the main assembly room, to gather in a separate room, and to wait for instructions from the facilitator. After they have left, the facilitator makes the following announcement to the remaining participants:

"In a few minutes, your reader will read the selected copy one time only, without repeating any word, phrase, or sentence. Be sensitive to any information that is read to you; if a command or instruction is given you, act accordingly. After the reading has been completed, you will be tested on the material that you have just heard. Consequently, you should listen carefully. You are not allowed to take notes during the reading."

The members of each group are instructed to spend the next fifteen minutes discussing the qualities needed to be a good listener while the facilitator, the readers, and the observers prepare for the activity.

---

[1]From J.R. Luthi, "Communicating Communication," in J.W. Pfeiffer and J.E. Jones (Eds.), *The 1978 Annual Handbook for Group Facilitators,* University Associates, 1978. The deterrents cited in the Luthi article are from R.G. Nichols, *Listening Is a Ten Part Skill,* Enterprise Publications, 1952.

IV. The facilitator leaves the main assembly room and joins the readers and observers. Each of these participants is given a copy of the I'm All Ears Reading Sheet and is asked to read the entire sheet. Questions are elicited and answered, and the facilitator coaches the readers as necessary while they practice their reading. In addition, the facilitator gives each observer a copy of the observer sheet and a pencil and explains that during the listening activity the observers are to follow the instructions on this handout. The observers also are encouraged to provide the readers with suggestions during the practice period. (Fifteen minutes.)

V. The facilitator, the readers, and the observers return to the main assembly room, and the readers and observers rejoin their groups.

VI. Each reader is instructed to begin reading. The facilitator monitors the groups to ensure that the participants are following instructions. (Five minutes.)

VII. After the readings have been concluded, each listener is given a copy of the I'm All Ears Retention Test and a pencil and is asked to work independently to complete the test. Each reader is instructed to join his or her group's observer at a separate table, and each of these dyads is asked to discuss quietly what happened during the previous step so that the observer can complete the observer sheet. (Ten minutes.)

VIII. Each listener is given a copy of the I'm All Ears Scoring Sheet and is instructed to determine his or her own score.

IX. The readers and observers are asked to return to their respective groups, and the observers are asked to share and discuss the contents of the completed observer sheets with their fellow members. (Twenty minutes.)

X. The facilitator reassembles the total group and leads a concluding discussion by asking the following questions:

1. How did you feel during this activity?

2. What did you do to help yourself retain and recall information?

3. What caused you the most trouble in listening to the material that was read?

4. What are some common distractions that cause faulty listening?

5. What did you learn about your own listening skills? about the listening skills of others?

6. How can distractions to listening be overcome? What is one thing that you can do to listen more effectively in the future?

Variations

I. The section entitled "Material To Be Read" in the reading sheet may be recorded on tape prior to the activity. Playing the recorded material for the participants eliminates the need for readers and allows all participants to hear the same oral delivery.

II. The facilitator may write a different script to be read to the participants. If the participants share a common profession, the script content may be material that is of interest to members of that profession.

III. The activity may be made competitive by announcing that the top-scoring individual(s) or group will be rewarded in some way.

Similar Structured Experience: *Vol. VII:* Structured Experience **251.**

Lecturette Sources: *'73 Annual,* p. 120: "Conditions Which Hinder Effective Communication"; *'78 Annual,* p. 123: "Communicating Communication."

Notes on the Use of "I'm All Ears":

Submitted by James I. Costigan and Sandra K. Tyson.

I'M ALL EARS READING SHEET

Instructions

While reading the "Material To Be Read" (below) to your group, make sure that you follow these instructions:

- Read as clearly and concisely as possible and loudly enough that all members of your group can hear you.
- Read the bracketed commands as if they were part of the story.
- Do *not* repeat any word, phrase, or sentence, even if your fellow members ask you to do so.
- Do *not* answer any questions.

You may *not* read or explain these instructions to your group.

Material To Be Read

Many college students combine their classroom work with on-the-job experience in businesses. Even though these students study and do research in the university library after attending classes and working, they still find several hours a day for recreation. Here is what a few representative students do in their spare time:

Phyllis Campbell is the editor of the bimonthly magazine, *Getting the Business,* published by and for the undergraduate students in the School of Business. Phyllis's previous editorial experience consisted of editing her high school yearbook. Now she finds it great fun writing about business issues and encouraging other students [wink at the person to your left] to write for the publication. She has formed an editorial committee on which members of the faculty [touch the person to your right] serve as advisors. The students who are members of this committee were selected to represent a variety of business interests, and it is their point of view that determines the magazine's policy and its ultimate editorial content. Other students function as reporters, feature writers, and illustrators. The magazine also has a business manager and pays its own way by selling advertising space to local fast-food shops, clothing stores, and movie theaters. Phyllis is not sure how much of her time she will devote to writing after she receives her college degree, but she knows [raise your hand and say "howdy"] that she is gaining valuable experience.

Another example of an active student who finds time for recreation is John Miller, who is the captain of the intramural swimming team sponsored by the School of Business. He supervises team practices in the university sports complex [hold hands with someone] and sees to it that members keep up to par on speed and form. Twice each year John arranges swim meets with the intramural squads sponsored by the School of Law and the School of Medicine. These meets are well attended by the students of the School of Business [look behind you], who cheer their classmates with genuine collegiate vigor.

Even among business students who are not members of university teams, participation in sports is an important pastime. For example, the physical-education department provides opportunities for all students to play basketball, tennis, and badminton, and the courts attract plenty of business students as "customers."

The School of Business also offers a program of social activities, primarily in the form of rock concerts, to provide relief from the stiff schedules of business and classroom work. For the most part, the students themselves have an opportunity to plan, organize [tap the shoulder of someone near you], and run these events, although, of course, faculty members are ready to help out if needed.

I'M ALL EARS OBSERVER SHEET

Instructions: Your task is to observe the behavior of the listeners in your group. After the reader has finished reading, he or she will join you to discuss what happened during the listening task; at that time you will write answers to the following questions. Then you and the reader will be asked to rejoin your group and to share and discuss the completed contents of this sheet.

1. How did the listeners prepare themselves to listen? What signs of attentiveness did they demonstrate?

2. As the reader proceeded, what did the listeners do to help themselves in the listening process? What changes in their behavior did you observe?

3. What seemed to hinder the listeners as they listened? What measures did they take to overcome these hindrances?

4. How would you describe the interaction between the reader and the listeners?

I'M ALL EARS RETENTION TEST

1. What is the name of the editor of the undergraduate business magazine?

2. What is the title of the magazine?

3. How often is it published?

For Items 4 and 5, list two of the magazine's three sources of advertising revenue.

4.

5.

6. How much time does the editor of the magazine plan to devote to writing after completing college?

7. What is the name of the captain of the intramural swimming team sponsored by the School of Business?

8. How many swim meets does the captain arrange each year?

9. Where does the School of Business' swimming team practice?

For Items 10 and 11, list the two intramural squads that serve as the opponents for the School of Business' swimming team.

10.

11.

For Items 12, 13, and 14, list the three sports that all students are afforded opportunities to play, even if they do not belong to university teams.

12.

13.

14.

15. What is the main form of social activity offered by the School of Business to provide relief from the stiff schedules of business and classroom work?

I'M ALL EARS SCORING SHEET

Answers

    1. Phyllis Campbell

    2. *Getting the Business*

    3. Bimonthly

  4, 5. Any two of the following: fast-food shops, clothing stores, and movie theaters

    6. She is not sure at the present time.

    7. John Miller

    8. Two

    9. In the university sports complex

 10, 11. Squads of the School of Law and the School of Medicine

12, 13, 14. Basketball, tennis, and badminton

   15. Rock concerts

Scale

  15 - Superior

13-14 - Excellent

11-12 - Good

 4-10 - Average

 2- 3 - Fair

 0- 1 - Poor

396. IN OTHER WORDS: BUILDING ORAL-COMMUNICATION SKILLS

Goals

I. To acquaint the participants with some useful tips regarding effective oral communication.

II. To allow the participants to practice translating long, written messages into short but accurate and effective oral ones.

III. To offer the participants an opportunity to give and receive feedback about the effectiveness of their translations and their delivery.

Group Size

A maximum of ten triads.

Time Required

Approximately one and one-half hours.

Materials

I. One copy of the In Other Words Communication Handout for each participant.

II. One copy each of In Other Words Translation Sheets A, B, and C for each participant.

III. A pencil for each participant.

IV. A clipboard or other portable writing surface for each participant.

Physical Setting

A room in which the triads can work without disturbing one another. Movable chairs should be provided for the participants.

Process

I. The facilitator explains the goals of the activity.

II. Each participant is given a copy of the In Other Words Communication Handout and is asked to read it. The facilitator leads a discussion of each of the tips presented in this handout, clarifying any points as necessary for the participants. (Twenty minutes.)

III. The facilitator instructs the participants to assemble into triads. Each participant is given one copy each of In Other Words Translation Sheets A, B, and C; a pencil; and a clipboard or other portable writing surface. The facilitator explains that one member of each triad is to concentrate on sheet A, another member is to concentrate on sheet B, and the third member is to concentrate on sheet C. Each participant is to work independently to translate the paragraph on his or her sheet into a message that is approximately half as long as the original message. This translation is to be written below the original paragraph on the sheet. (Ten minutes.)

IV. The facilitator explains that within each triad all three members are to read the paragraph on sheet A silently; the member who translated this paragraph is to review his or her translation at the same time. Then the member who translated the paragraph is to turn his or her sheet face down and to deliver the translation orally. The facilitator stipulates that the oral translation need not be a word-for-word reproduction of the one that was written, but that the member delivering it should make a conscious effort to use the tips presented in the communication handout. The other two members are to listen carefully to the translation; to evaluate it for accuracy, brevity, effectiveness of statement, and use of the tips presented in the communication handout; and to provide the first member with this feedback. Then all three members are to discuss other ways in which the paragraph could have been translated. This procedure is to be followed until all three members have translated their paragraphs, received feedback about their translations, and participated in a discussion of alternative translations. After ensuring that the participants understand the task, the facilitator asks them to begin. (Forty-five minutes.)

V. The facilitator reassembles the total group for a concluding discussion. The following questions are asked:

1. What was easy or difficult about writing the translation? What was easy or difficult about delivering the translation orally?

2. What common steps did each member of your triad take in translating?

3. How did the translations differ with regard to member input? What might account for these differences?

4. Which affected the presentations more: the writing of the translation or its delivery? How did the writing and the delivery combine in total effect?

5. What are some "dos" and "don'ts" for translating written messages into oral form? What other generalizations can be made about oral communication?

6. What new ideas can you incorporate into your interactions with others to build your oral-communication skills further?

Variations

I. The participants may be instructed to translate the paragraphs orally without writing their translations beforehand.

II. The participants may be asked to translate and deliver messages that are already concise.

III. If the participants share a common profession, the facilitator may replace the translation sheets with paragraphs whose content reflects issues of concern to members of that profession.

IV. The activity may be altered to focus on improving the participants' written-communication skills. In this case the facilitator should replace the existing communication handout with one that presents tips for effective writing.

Notes on the Use of "In Other Words":

Based on T.W. Goad, *Delivering Effective Training,* University Associates, 1982.

Structured Experience   396

IN OTHER WORDS COMMUNICATION HANDOUT

Here are some tips to help you to communicate orally with greater effectiveness.

1. Avoid sexist language, regardless of whether your audience includes members of both sexes.
2. Use correct grammar. Never talk down to any audience.
3. Avoid slang and jargon. Clear, precise, simple language is better.
4. Avoid saying "er," "ah," and "umm."
5. Speak up. Vary your pitch, but always speak distinctly and enunciate carefully.
6. Monitor your pace as you speak. Avoid speaking too rapidly or too slowly.
7. Establish eye contact with your listeners so that they will listen and respond to what you are saying and so that you can see whether they are understanding you.
8. If you use gestures while you are speaking, make sure that they are appropriate to what you are saying.

Adapted from T.W. Goad, *Delivering Effective Training,* University Associates, 1982.

IN OTHER WORDS TRANSLATION SHEET A

Misunderstandings between persons can occur because of faulty assumptions people make about communication. Two such faulty assumptions are (1) *"you"* always know what *"I"* mean and (2) *"I"* should always know what *"you"* mean. The premise seems to be that since people live or work together, they are or should be able to read each other's minds. Some people believe that since they are transparent to themselves, they are transparent to others as well. "Since I exist, you should understand me," they seem to be saying. Persons who make this assumption often presume that they communicate clearly if they simply say what they please. In fact, they often leave the persons listening to them confused and guessing about the message being communicated. Misunderstanding is common because clarity of communication does not happen.

From M.R. Chartier, "Clarity of Expression in Interpersonal Communication," in J.W. Pfeiffer and J.E. Jones, *The 1976 Annual Handbook for Group Facilitators,* University Associates, 1976.

Structured Experience 396

IN OTHER WORDS TRANSLATION SHEET B

Clarity of communication is influenced by the extent to which those listening and those sending are aware of their communication skills. It is possible to evaluate the assumptions one holds about his or her ability to communicate messages. Persons with careless speech-communication habits are often convinced that they are successful communicators because they are able to open their mouths and utter a stream of words. Actual skills in interpersonal communication, however, are quite different. An accurate assessment of one's own communication weaknesses and strengths is important. Often, strengths can be maximized and weaknesses improved. One person may have a sparkling personality that aids him or her in communication. Another may have a way with words. Yet another may be able to communicate in such a way that others feel he or she understands them.

From M.R. Chartier, "Clarity of Expression in Interpersonal Communication," in J.W. Pfeiffer and J.E. Jones, *The 1976 Annual Handbook for Group Facilitators,* University Associates, 1976.

IN OTHER WORDS TRANSLATION SHEET C

The context of communication is important in determining the amount of accuracy needed or possible between persons in a given situation. How much clarity can be achieved is somewhat determined by the persons' communication skills, the number of communication channels available to the person sending, how much repetition he or she can incorporate into the message, and the nature of the relationship between the persons communicating. Attempting to communicate with a person in another room presents more difficulties for the clarification process than does speaking face-to-face. In short, the speaker needs to develop a realistic expectation for the degree of clarity obtainable in a given context.

From M. R. Chartier, "Clarity of Expression in Interpersonal Communication," in J. W. Pfeiffer and J. E. Jones, *The 1976 Annual Handbook for Group Facilitators,* University Associates, 1976.

Structured Experience   396

397. TAKING RESPONSIBILITY: PRACTICE IN COMMUNICATING ASSUMPTIONS

Goals

    I. To develop the participants' understanding of the effects of assumptions on oral communication.

    II. To offer the participants an opportunity to practice devising comments that demonstrate their willingness to assume responsibility for stating their assumptions.

Group Size

    Any number of triads.

Time Required

    Two hours.

Materials

    I. A copy of the Taking Responsibility Theory Sheet for each participant.

    II. A copy of the Taking Responsibility Work Sheet for each participant.

    III. A pencil for each participant.

Physical Setting

    A room that is large enough to allow the triads to work without disturbing one another. Chairs and writing surfaces should be provided for the participants.

Process

    I. The facilitator explains the goals of the activity.

    II. Each participant is given a copy of the Taking Responsibility Theory Sheet and is asked to read this handout. (Ten minutes.)

    III. The facilitator leads a discussion about the contents of the theory sheet, eliciting and answering questions as necessary. (Fifteen minutes.)

IV. Each participant is given a copy of the Taking Responsibility Work Sheet and a pencil and is asked to complete the sheet. (Thirty minutes.)

V. The participants are assembled into triads. The members of each triad are asked to share their completed sheets with one another and to discuss the underlying assumptions as well as the merits of each member's rewritten comment for each item. (Forty-five minutes.)

VI. The total group is reassembled for a concluding discussion. The facilitator asks the following questions:

1. Which comments on the work sheet were easy to rewrite? Which were difficult? How do you account for the difference in difficulty?

2. What common assumptions did you discover on the work sheet? On what points did you and your fellow triad members agree and disagree during your discussion? What part did your own assumptions play in these agreements and disagreements?

3. What might be the consequences of failing to state assumptions specifically when conversing with others? What might be the consequences of stating assumptions specifically?

4. What seem to be the major assumptions that are left unspoken in your home or work environment? How might these assumptions be communicated openly? What might happen if this open communication were to take place?

Variations

I. After Step VI the participants may be asked to return to their triads to work on ways to state assumptions clearly in their home and/or work environments.

II. If the participants share a particular line of work, the comments on the work sheet may be rewritten to reflect assumptions that are common to that line of work.

III. The participants may be asked to role play situations involving some of the comments on their work sheet before and after these comments are rewritten. Subsequently, reactions are compared.

Similar Structured Experiences: *Volume VI:* Structured Experience **202**; *Vol. VII:* **250**; *Vol. VIII:* **307.**

Suggested Instrument: *'74 Annual*, p. 97: "Interpersonal Communication Inventory."

Lecturette Sources: *'73 Annual,* p. 120: "Conditions Which Hinder Effective Communication"; *'74 Annual,* p. 125: "Five Components Contributing to Effective Interpersonal Communications," p. 129: "Making Requests Through Metacommunication"; *'78 Annual,* p. 119: "Communication Effectiveness: Active Listening and Sending Feeling Messages," p. 123: "Communicating Communication"; *'79 Annual,* p. 128: "Anybody with Eyes Can See the Facts!"; *'80 Annual,* p. 127: "The Four-Communication-Styles Approach"; *'81 Annual,* p. 113: "Defensive and Supportive Communication," p. 124: "Kenepathy."

Notes on the Use of "Taking Responsibility":

Submitted by Gilles L. Talbot.

TAKING RESPONSIBILITY THEORY SHEET

It is a characteristic of human nature to try to assess or "make sense of" human behavior. However, the assumptions we make about the behavior of others are not necessarily what others *are*; instead, our assumptions are reflections of our own values and beliefs. When conversing with another person, it is important to remember this fact, to clarify assumptions, and to be willing to accept at least some of the responsibility for any ambiguity in the communication.

Here are some suggestions about ways to take responsibility and to clarify assumptions when communicating with another person:

1. Specify the behavior(s) on which the assumption is based: "Your facial expression suggests to me that you're confused" rather than "Are you following what I'm saying?"

2. If your assumption compares the listener's behavior with that of other members of a reference group, state what the group is and exactly how the behavior compares: "The other members of the department always submit their weekly production reports on Monday, and each of your last four reports wasn't submitted until Thursday" rather than "You don't submit your weekly production reports promptly."

3. If your assumption is based on your own expectation of the listener's behavior, state that expectation specifically; do not assume that the listener knows the details of your expectation: "I'm expecting that report next Monday at 4:00. Can we agree on that?" rather than "Is that report going to be done on time?"

4. Elicit feedback about your assumption; ask the listener to tell you whether the assumption is accurate: "Am I correct in assuming that you've already begun writing the report that's due next Monday?"

TAKING RESPONSIBILITY WORK SHEET

Instructions: For each of the following comments, (1) write the underlying assumption, and (2) employ one or more of the four suggestions on the Taking Responsibility Theory Sheet to rewrite the comment so that it reflects an effort to take responsibility and to communicate assumptions clearly.

1. "Can't you work under pressure?"

2. "You're not listening to me."

3. "Will you work overtime Friday?"

4. "Joyce, what have you done with the production figures?"

5. "Get me the copyright file! And hurry up!"

6. "Don't you like the boss?"

7. "How are you going to get us out of this mess?"

8. "Are you getting all of this down in writing?"

9. "Why are you mad at me?"

10. "You've never appreciated my work."

398. PASS IT ON: SIMULATING ORGANIZATIONAL COMMUNICATION

Goals

  I. To enhance the participants' understanding of the complexity of oral communication patterns within an organization.

  II. To illustrate what happens to messages that are transmitted orally through several different channels within an organization.

  III. To explore ways to improve oral communication within an organization.

Group Size

  Twenty to thirty-two participants.

Time Required

  One hour and forty-five minutes.

Materials

  I. One copy of the Pass It On Instruction Sheet for each participant.

  II. One copy of the Pass It On Observer Sheet for each observer.

  III. A pencil for each observer.

  IV. A clipboard or other portable writing surface for each observer.

  V. One copy of the Pass It On Messages (to be used only by the facilitator).

  VI. A name tag for each participant. Prior to conducting the activity, the facilitator labels these tags as follows:

    1. One tag labeled "President";

    2. Three to five tags labeled "Executive Vice President";

    3. Three to five tags labeled "Vice President";

    4. Three to five tags labeled "Manager";

    5. Three to five tags labeled "Production Worker";

    6. Three to five tags labeled "Operations Worker";

    7. Two to four tags labeled "Observer"; and

    8. Two tags labeled "Recorder."

A different version of this structured experience appeared in L. C. Lederman and L. P. Stewart, "One Day in an Organization," in *SIMCORP Participants' Manual*, Total Research Corporation, 1983. Adapted with the permission of the authors.

VII. Six newsprint signs designating the areas of the room assigned to the various groups. Prior to conducting the activity, the facilitator prepares these signs with the following labels (one per sign): "President," "Executive Vice Presidents," "Vice Presidents," "Managers," "Production Workers," and "Operations Workers."

VIII. A newsprint reproduction of the organizational hierarchy illustrated on the instruction sheet. The facilitator prepares this reproduction prior to conducting the activity.

IX. Masking tape for posting newsprint.

X. Two newsprint flip charts and two felt-tipped markers (one chart and marker placed at the president's station and another chart and marker placed at the operations workers' station).

Physical Setting

A large room that will allow the participants to move back and forth freely. The signs designating the stations for the organizational groups should be taped to the wall in different areas of the room. One flip chart and felt-tipped marker should be placed at the president's station, and the other flip chart and marker should be placed at the operations workers' station. The newsprint reproduction of the organizational hierarchy should be taped to the wall in such a way that it can be viewed by all participants.

Process

I. The facilitator explains the goals of the activity.

II. The participants are assigned roles for the simulation: one president, three to five executive vice presidents, three to five vice presidents, three to five managers, three to five production workers, three to five operations workers, two to four observers, and two recorders. Name tags are distributed. The groups that comprise the organizational hierarchy are stationed at different areas within the room; one recorder is stationed near the president, and one is stationed near the operations workers; and the observers are stationed in different places so that they can observe the activity from different vantage points.

III. Each participant is given a copy of the Pass It On Instruction Sheet and is asked to read this sheet. Each observer is also given a copy of the observer sheet, a pencil, and a clipboard or other portable writing surface and is asked to read the observer sheet. The facilitator elicits and answers questions about the activity. (Fifteen minutes.)

IV. The facilitator gives the organizational groups their assigned messages one by one, each time reciting the group's message carefully but so that the other groups cannot hear the content; no participant is allowed to see his or her group's written message or to write the recited message. In addition, each recorder is instructed to receive messages from the appropriate participant(s) and to record these messages *word for word* on newsprint; the facilitator emphasizes to each recorder that the received messages must not be translated into the recorder's own words.

V. The participants are instructed to begin the simulation. The facilitator monitors their actions to ensure that the flow of communication is as described on the instruction sheet.

VI. The facilitator stops the simulation when all messages have been recorded on newsprint. (The recorder stationed near the president will have recorded three messages, and the recorder stationed near the operations workers will have recorded four messages.)

VII. The total group is reassembled, and the observers are asked to share the content of their observer sheets.

VIII. The facilitator leads a discussion of the activity. The following questions are asked:

1. What reactions did you have to the conveying and receiving of messages? What difficulties did you experience? How did you compensate for these difficulties? What surprises did you experience?

2. What are some words you would use to describe the oral communication within the organization portrayed in this simulation? How does your description compare with the way in which oral communication occurs in your own organization?

3. What can you generalize about oral communication among hierarchies within an organization?

4. How might oral communication within an organization be improved? What would have to happen in order to generate this improvement?

5. What could you personally do to simplify the oral-communication process in your own organization? How might you increase clarity and reduce distortion in communication?

Variations

I. After Step VIII the participants may be asked to use the improvements they have suggested to convey different messages.

II. If the participants share a common profession, the facilitator may devise different messages that reflect that profession.

III. To shorten the activity, the number of organizational levels may be reduced.

Similar Structured Experiences: *Volume II:* Structured Experience **28**; *'79 Annual:* **241**.

Lecturette Sources: *'73 Annual,* p. 120: "Conditions Which Hinder Effective Communication"; *'74 Annual,* p. 125: "Five Components Contributing to Effective Interpersonal Communications," p. 150: "Communication Patterns in Organization Structure"; *'78 Annual,* p. 123: "Communicating Communication."

Notes on the Use of "Pass It On":

Submitted by Linda Costigan Lederman and Lea P. Stewart.

PASS IT ON INSTRUCTION SHEET

Instructions: During the upcoming activity, you and your fellow participants will take part in a simulation of the flow of organizational communication. If you have been assigned a role within the organizational hierarchy, you will be conveying and receiving certain messages. To begin the activity, the facilitator will instruct each group separately about the message that it is to convey, and one of the members of this group will deliver the message *orally* to one of the members of the group that is to receive the message. Consult the organizational hierarchy illustrated below and the copy that follows to determine the flow of messages.

Organizational Hierarchy

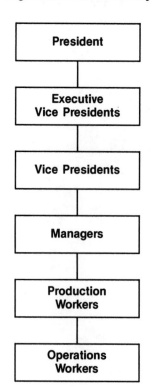

President

The president conveys his or her assigned message to and receives messages from the *executive vice presidents*. Each time the president receives a message, he or she recites this message to the recorder standing nearby, who then records the message *word for word* on newsprint.

Executive Vice Presidents

The executive vice presidents convey their assigned message to the *vice presidents*. They receive a message from the president and convey it to the vice presidents, and they receive messages from the vice presidents and convey these to the president.

Vice Presidents

The vice presidents convey their assigned message to the *managers*. They receive messages from the executive vice presidents and convey them to the managers, and they receive messages from the managers and convey them to the executive vice presidents.

Managers

The managers convey their assigned message to the *vice presidents and the production workers*. They receive messages from the vice presidents and convey them to the production workers, and they receive messages from the production workers and convey them to the vice presidents.

Production Workers

The production workers convey their assigned message to the *managers*. They receive messages from the managers and convey them to the operations workers, and they receive a message from the operations workers and convey it to the managers.

Operations Workers

The operations workers convey their assigned message to and receive messages from the *production workers*. Each time a message is received, the operations worker who received it recites the message to the recorder standing nearby, who then records the message *word for word* on newsprint.

PASS IT ON OBSERVER SHEET

Instructions: During the upcoming activity, you are to observe the participants' interactions carefully and write answers to the following questions. Later you will be asked to share these questions and your answers with the total group. If you need clarification of this assignment, consult the facilitator in private; do *not* share the content of this sheet with the participants who are involved in the simulation.

1. How are the participants choosing to convey and receive messages?

2. What types of feelings and reactions are the participants displaying?

3. What distortions of messages are occurring in the exchange? What are the participants doing to reduce distortion and/or increase clarity?

4. What similarities and differences are becoming apparent among groups as the participants convey and receive messages? What patterns are developing within and among groups? What significance do these patterns have?

PASS IT ON MESSAGES

President's Message

This year's company picnic will be held on Saturday, May 1. All employees and their families are cordially invited.

Executive Vice Presidents' Message

Because extra cash is available at present, it has been decided to make some improvements to the company's building. The exterior of the building will be painted in April, and the interior will be painted in June.

Vice Presidents' Message

The company is instituting a system to reward employees whose performance is exceptional. Each month one employee will be chosen as the recipient, and this individual will be given $250 during a special award ceremony.

Managers' Message

All production and operations workers are being asked to work an extra two hours per shift for the next two weeks so that the company can fill a large customer order.

Production Workers' Message

The production workers would like a company-paid policy of disability insurance to be added to the employee-benefits package.

Operations Workers' Message

The operations workers would like to have four more vending machines installed: two machines that dispense soft drinks and two that dispense snacks.

399. THE HUMAN BANK ACCOUNT: PRACTICING SELF-AFFIRMATION

Goals

I. To increase the participants' awareness of their own and others' ability to affect their self-concepts.

II. To offer the participants an opportunity to practice assuming control of their self-concepts and making self-affirming responses to comments made by others.

Group Size

Five to eight triads.

Time Required

Two hours.

Materials

I. Blank paper and a pencil for each participant.

II. A clipboard or other portable writing surface for each participant.

III. A newsprint flip chart and a felt-tipped marker.

IV. Masking tape for posting newsprint.

Physical Setting

A room large enough so that the triads can work without disturbing one another. Movable chairs should be provided for the participants.

Process

I. The facilitator introduces the concept of the "human bank account" by making the following comments:[1]

---

[1]Adapted from W.C. Boshear and K.G. Albrecht, "Human Bank Account," in *Understanding People: Models and Concepts,* University Associates, 1977.

"The term 'human bank account' is used to represent the life pattern of basing one's self-esteem on the opinions, attitudes, and evaluations of others. An individual who behaves like a human bank account feels good when praised, feels hurt and inferior when reprimanded, and feels angry when insulted or verbally attacked. Such a person allows others to raise or lower his or her feelings of self-worth and forfeits the power to influence those feelings.

"The comparison to a bank account is particularly appropriate in that others are allowed to make 'deposits' to and 'withdrawals' from such a person. A more positive life pattern consists of maintaining one's own 'balance' of good feelings and self-acceptance."

II. The facilitator distributes blank paper, pencils, and clipboards or other portable writing surfaces and then writes the following incomplete sentences on newsprint:

1. The comments that people make to me that increase my feelings of self-worth are. . . .

2. The comments that people make to me that decrease my feelings of self-worth are. . . .

Each participant is instructed to reproduce the two sentences on paper, completing each with at least three sample comments. (Fifteen minutes.)

III. The participants are asked to assemble into triads and to take turns sharing their completed sentences with one another. The facilitator explains that each comment that increases self-worth as well as each comment that decreases self-worth should be considered separately; after the participant reads a comment, all three group members are to work to devise responses to the comment that indicate a strong reliance on one's own positive self-concept rather than on altering one's self-concept in accordance with the comment. The facilitator provides the following examples of a positive comment and an appropriate response as well as a negative comment and an appropriate response:

Comment: "I think you made a really outstanding presentation at the meeting yesterday."

Response: "Thanks. That's good to hear. I was pleased with it, too. Could you give me any specifics about what you particularly liked?"

Comment: "That was the worst proposal I've ever seen."

Response: "I'm surprised. I thought it was rather good. Perhaps you have some specific suggestions that I could consider to make my next proposal better."

It is also stipulated that the participant who reads the original comment is to keep a written record of all responses. After clarifying these instructions as necessary, the facilitator asks the triads to begin. (Thirty minutes.)

Structured Experience   **399**

IV. After the triads have completed their work, the facilitator reassembles the total group. One positive comment and response and one negative comment and response are elicited from each triad, written on newsprint, and posted; then opinions are elicited regarding whether the responses are suitable and why. The participants are also asked to contribute additional responses to specific comments that might be appropriate and self-affirming, and these responses are recorded on newsprint. (Thirty minutes.)

V. New triads are assembled for the purpose of practicing self-affirming responses. The facilitator explains that one member within each triad is to select one positive comment from those listed on newsprint and to make that comment to another triad member, and the recipient of the comment is to make a self-affirming response; then the third triad member is to select a negative comment and to make that comment to the same recipient, and again the recipient is to make a self-affirming response. The facilitator clarifies that this procedure is to be followed until each participant has heard and responded to two comments. The participants are told that they are to respond to the comments they hear in as spontaneous a fashion as possible and without using the responses posted on newsprint. The facilitator also stipulates that after each triad has completed the entire procedure, the members are to take turns stating an adjective that describes their feelings at the moment. After clarifying these instructions as necessary, the facilitator tells the triads to begin. (Twenty minutes.)

VI. The facilitator reassembles the total group and asks the following questions:

1. How did you feel after making self-affirming responses to the comments made by your fellow triad members? What was easy and/or difficult about making these responses?

2. How did you feel after hearing self-affirming responses to your own comments?

3. How did this experience affect your relationship with your fellow triad members? How did it affect your image of yourself?

4. What have you learned about maintaining a positive self-concept? What are the "truths" that emerge from this activity?

5. How can you sustain this process of maintaining your own "balance"? What are some sources of support that you can use? What are some obstacles that you might face? How can you overcome these obstacles?

Variations

I. During Step V the members of each triad may be instructed to devise their own comments instead of using those written on newsprint.

II. After Step V the members of each triad may be asked to make comments to one another based on their present knowledge of one another. After such comments are made, the members practice self-affirming responses.

III. After Step VI the participants may be asked to return to their triads for a follow-up self-affirming activity. For example, they may be instructed to make lists of their positive traits.

IV. The activity may be altered to focus on responding to *either* positive or negative comments exclusively.

Similar Structured Experiences: *'76 Annual:* Structured Experience **181**; *Vol. VIII:* **306**.

Notes on the Use of "The Human Bank Account":

Based on W. C. Boshear and K. G. Albrecht, "Human Bank Account," in *Understanding People: Models and Concepts,* University Associates, 1977.

400. THE DECENT BUT PESKY CO-WORKER: DEVELOPING CONTRACTING SKILLS

Goals

I. To acquaint the participants with the significance and usefulness of contracting as a means of facilitating the helping process.

II. To develop the participants' understanding of and skills in contracting.

Group Size

Any number of dyads.

Time Required

Approximately one and one-half hours.

Materials

I. One copy of The Decent but Pesky Co-Worker Role Sheet A for each dyad.

II. One copy of The Decent but Pesky Co-Worker Role Sheet B for each dyad.

III. One copy of The Decent but Pesky Co-Worker Theory Sheet for each participant.

Physical Setting

A room with plenty of space so that the dyads can enact their role plays without disturbing one another.

Process

I. The facilitator tells the participants that they are to be involved in a role play.

II. The participants are instructed to assemble into dyads. One member of each dyad receives a copy of role sheet A, and the other member receives a copy of role sheet B. The facilitator asks each participant to read his or her role sheet and to spend a few minutes thinking about how to play the assigned role. In addition, the facilitator emphasizes the importance of maintaining roles during the role play and cautions the participants *not* to share the contents of their role sheets with one another. (Ten minutes.)

III. The facilitator instructs the dyads to begin their role plays. (Ten minutes.)

IV. The participants are instructed to stop their role plays. The members of each dyad are asked to discuss what they think was happening during the role play and what might have been done differently to improve the situation for both members. Again, the participants are cautioned not to discuss the particulars of their agendas as described on the role sheets. (Ten minutes.)

V. The total group is reconvened, and the facilitator elicits comments from the participants about the content of their dyadic discussions. (Ten minutes.)

VI. Copies of The Decent but Pesky Co-Worker Theory Sheet are distributed, and the participants are asked to read this sheet. Then the facilitator leads a discussion of the handout's contents, clarifying points as necessary and relating them to the comments made during Step V. (Twenty minutes.)

VII. The participants are instructed to reassemble into their dyads and to start their role plays again from the beginning, this time using the contracting process and incorporating what they have learned from the activity to this point. (Fifteen minutes.)

VIII. The facilitator stops the role plays and reconvenes the total group. The following questions are asked:

1. What were the differences between the first and second role plays? How do you account for these differences?

2. What new questions did you ask during the second role play? What new statements did you make?

3. How productive were the two role plays in terms of problem solving? How satisfying were the resolutions of the two role plays?

4. How would you characterize your relationship with your partner during the second role play? In what ways were the two of you interacting differently from the way you interacted during the first role play?

5. What have you learned about the skills necessary for contracting? How can you relate what you have learned to what happens in your private life and in your own organization with regard to problem solving?

6. What steps will you take the next time you want help from a co-worker or friend? What steps will you take when someone asks for help from you?

7. What might be some other uses of the contracting process? What might be the benefits of using contracting in various situations?

Variations

I. During Step VII the members of each dyad may be asked to switch roles.

II. An observer may be asked to join each dyad. When the members of the dyad experience difficulties, the observer may be instructed to help in the contracting process by serving as a third-party consultant.

III. The facilitator may devise several different sets of role sheets based on different co-worker problems. Subsequently, during processing, the participants are asked to compare the effects of the different problems on the contracting process.

Lecturette Sources: *'78 Annual,* p. 138: "Contracting: A Process and a Tool"; *'82 Annual,* p. 147: "Checkpoints in the Contracting Process."

Notes on the Use of "The Decent but Pesky Co-Worker":

Submitted by Larry Porter.

THE DECENT BUT PESKY CO-WORKER ROLE SHEET A

For the past two months, one of your co-workers has been in the habit of visiting your office once or twice a week to complain about personal financial problems. You have tried to be as understanding and as helpful as possible and even have suggested some actions that the co-worker might take to alleviate the situation; however, despite your efforts, the financial problems remain the same, and your efforts to complete your work in peace continue to be thwarted by your co-worker's visits.

You want to be helpful and to remain on friendly terms with your co-worker, but you are tired of hearing the same complaint repeatedly and you are beginning to be extremely concerned about the amount of time these conversations take away from your work.

Here the co-worker comes again. Quick! Think of how you can manage the conversation in such a way that you are friendly and helpful to this person and can attend to your own needs as well.

THE DECENT BUT PESKY CO-WORKER ROLE SHEET B

You are in a real bind. For some time now, you have been experiencing serious financial problems. A couple of months ago you confided in one of your co-workers about this situation and how serious it is. Since then you have visited the co-worker's office once or twice a week to discuss your financial problems, but so far this person has failed to suggest anything helpful. However, you admire the co-worker's problem-solving ability and believe that eventually this person will give you the "right answer."

Lately you have begun to feel desperate about your financial future. You are on your way to the co-worker's office now to ask for help again.

THE DECENT BUT PESKY CO-WORKER THEORY SHEET

Contracting is a procedure frequently used by professionals in their dealings with clients. It is a process by which both the professional and the client become aware of and agree to how the work in question will be done, what their relationship will be like, what methods and resources will be used, what the objectives and standards for measuring success will be, and so forth.

This process is an important part of any helper/helpee relationship—professional or nonprofessional—and often has a direct bearing on the success or failure of the "consultation." It establishes important understandings and guidelines and clarifies what the potential "client" wants from the "consultation." As is true with legal contracts, there should be a "consideration" for each party; in other words, each should be rewarded in some way. In addition, both parties should have a clear understanding about the contract and should have the freedom either to accept it or not. Ideally, the contract should be "open" in the sense that it can be renegotiated at any point, subject to the approval of both parties.

In a situation such as that involved in "The Decent but Pesky Co-Worker," the worker who serves as consultant might ask an initial contracting question like "How do you think I can be helpful to you?" The discussion generated by this question can be useful in clearing away a lot of assumptions and hidden agendas. Once this question has been satisfactorily answered—with both parties in agreement about what is being asked for and what the "consultant" can agree to deliver—the "consultant" might well ask other basic contracting questions: How much time do you think we will need? What have you tried already? How will we know if this consultation has been helpful? What do *I* (as "consultant") want from the consultation? In addition, the question of confidentiality may need to be addressed as well as other ethical issues, such as whether the "consultant" will be asked to take sides in the situation or to manipulate someone or something.

Contracting can be extremely useful in relatively informal, personal situations. In professional relationships its importance is much greater, and many more questions need to be raised and negotiated before the work can begin.[1] The clearer and more acceptable the contract to both parties, the greater the chances for the success of the consultative venture.

---

[1]See, for example, F. L. Ulschak, "Contracting: A Process and a Tool," in J. W. Pfeiffer and J. E. Jones (Eds.), *The 1978 Annual Handbook for Group Facilitators,* University Associates, 1978.

401. CHOOSE ME: DEVELOPING POWER WITHIN A GROUP

Goals

I. To explore issues related to power and influence within a group.

II. To offer each participant an opportunity to influence the other members of his or her group.

III. To allow the participants to give and receive feedback about their personal approaches to developing power and influence within a group.

Group Size

Three to five groups of five to seven each.

Time Required

Approximately two hours and fifteen minutes.

Materials

Blank paper and a pencil for each participant.

Physical Setting

A room with plenty of space for each group so that its members may make oral presentations to one another and engage in discussions without disturbing the other groups. A chair and a writing surface should be provided for each participant.

Process

I. The participants are assembled into groups of five to seven each.

II. The goals of the activity are explained.

III. The facilitator states that each group is to select a leader and clarifies the sequence of events whereby each group is to make its selection: Each member is to prepare a self-nominating presentation, making the best case that he or she can for being selected as the group's leader. The members are to take turns making their presentations to the group. Using all information available to them, the group members are to engage in their selection process. Then, under the guidance of the newly selected leader, the members are to prepare a report on their selection process. Subsequently, each group is to share its report with the total group.

IV. Each participant is given blank paper and a pencil for the purpose of making notes, if desired, while preparing his or her presentation. The participants are instructed to spend five minutes on their preparations and to restrict their presentations to a maximum of three minutes each.

V. The facilitator asks the members of each group to begin the presentation process. The participants are encouraged to listen carefully to each presentation and to take notes about each member's qualifications if they wish. (Three minutes *per presentation.*)

VI. Each group is instructed to use the data presented by the members to select its leader. The facilitator emphasizes that volunteering, choosing rotating leaders, opting to share leadership responsibilities, and deciding not to choose a leader are unacceptable approaches.

VII. After the choices have been made, the members of each group are asked to provide one another with feedback: One member at a time receives feedback from every other member regarding the effectiveness of the approach that he or she used to develop power and influence during Steps V and VI. (Twenty minutes.)

VIII. Each leader is instructed to lead his or her group in preparing an oral report on the group's selection process and deciding who is to present this report. (Thirty minutes.)

IX. The facilitator reassembles the total group and asks the groups to take turns reporting. (Twenty minutes.)

X. The facilitator leads a discussion about the activity, asking the following questions:

1. How did you feel about having to present yourself as a leader to your group? On what basis did you make your choice of characteristics to present to the group?

2. What do the things you chose to say about yourself and the way you chose to say them have to do with your concept of power and influence?

3. How would you describe your group's concept of power and influence as illustrated in the group's process of choosing a leader?

4. From your individual decisions and your group's operation, what can you generalize about power and influence in a group?

5. What are some specific ways to gain power in a group? How can power be lost or forfeited?

6. What can you do in the future to exert your power and influence more effectively in your home life or in your organization?

Variation

This activity may be altered to be used for the purpose of giving and receiving feedback related to leadership abilities or assertiveness.

Lecturette Source: *'76 Annual*, p. 139: "Power."

Notes on the Use of "Choose Me":

Submitted by Larry Porter.

402. POWER AND AFFECTION EXCHANGE: SHARING FEELINGS

Goals

I. To offer the participants an opportunity to express their feelings for one another.

II. To explore the participants' feelings about power and affection.

Group Size

Twenty to twenty-five members of an intact group.

Time Required

Approximately two hours.

Materials

I. Ten 3″ x 5″ index cards for each participant. Five of these cards should be of one color to designate them as "power" cards, and the other five should be of another color to designate them as "affection" cards. (In order to differentiate the cards in the "Process" section of this activity, the "power" cards are referred to as white and the "affection" cards are referred to as pink. The facilitator may choose any two colors that he or she wishes.)

II. A pencil for each participant.

III. A newsprint flip chart and a felt-tipped marker.

Physical Setting

A room with enough floor space for the participants to move around freely.

Process

I. The goals of the activity are introduced.

II. Each participant is given five white cards, five pink cards, and a pencil.

III. The facilitator explains the card-exchanging procedure as follows:

"Your white cards represent power, and your pink cards represent affection. In a few minutes, you will write your name on each of your pink affection cards; you will *not* write your name on any of the white power cards. Then you will be asked to begin a process of distributing the cards to your fellow group members. No talking will be allowed during this exchange period. You may give pink cards to those members for whom you feel affection, and you may give white cards to those members who you feel will make the best use of power. What you do with your cards, however, is entirely up to you: For example, if you want to keep them all and not participate in the exchange, you may do so; if you want to give several to the same person, you may also do that. In addition, you need not keep any cards you receive; if you wish, you may give them to someone else. Keep in mind that this means your affection and power cards may end up in the hands of people you did not intend to receive them.

"After the card transactions have been completed, those who are holding the power cards will vote on a way to show the affection that has been indicated by the distribution of the affection cards; each power card entitles the person holding it to one vote."

IV. The facilitator elicits and answers questions about the procedure and ensures that the participants understand it fully.

V. The following questions are asked:

1. How will you feel if you cannot give a card to every person you would like?

2. How will you feel if you receive no cards?

3. How will you feel if you give a card to someone who then gives it to another person?

4. What concerns or fears do you have about participating in this activity?

(Ten minutes.)

VI. The participants are told to write their names on their affection cards. Then the facilitator asks them to stand up and begin the exchange period and reminds them that they are not to talk to one another during this period.

VII. After all transactions have been completed, the participants are asked to be seated. The facilitator asks the following questions:

1. What happened to you during the exchange period?

2. How are you feeling at this moment?

3. How do you feel about the cards you received?

4. How did you feel about giving cards to others?

5. What surprises did you experience in giving cards? What surprises did you experience in receiving them?

(Thirty minutes.)

Structured Experience   402

VIII. The facilitator asks the participants who hold power cards to volunteer suggestions about how the affection represented by the pink cards should be shown. These suggestions are written on newsprint, and each participant who holds power cards is instructed to vote on the one suggestion that he or she likes best. Those with power cards are reminded that each card entitles the holder to one vote. (Ten minutes.)

IX. The results of the vote are announced, and the participants are instructed to carry out the chosen procedure for showing affection. (Twenty minutes.[1])

X. The facilitator reassembles the total group and leads a concluding discussion by asking the following questions:

1. How did you feel about using the chosen method for showing affection?
2. How do you feel about the way power was handled in choosing the method?
3. What insights have you gained about displaying and receiving displays of affection? What have you learned about displays of power?
4. How can you use what you have learned at home or at work? What might you do differently as a result of this activity?

Variations

I. The participants may be asked to write suggestions on their power cards of ways in which they feel affection should be shown.

II. A rule may be established that the participants are not allowed to give away the cards they receive.

III. After Step IX the participants may be asked to show affection in any way with which they feel comfortable.

Similar Structured Experience: *Volume V:* Structured Experience **167.**

---

[1]The time indicated for this step is an approximation only; it varies according to the procedure chosen for showing affection.

Notes on the Use of "Power and Affection Exchange":

The origin of this structured experience is unknown. This version was submitted by Gustave J. Rath.

403. YEARBOOK: POSITIVE GROUP FEEDBACK

Goals

   I. To allow the members of an ongoing group to give and receive positive feedback about their perceived roles within the group.

   II. To enhance the members' appreciation of themselves and one another.

   III. To help the members to determine ways in which group functioning might be improved in the future.

Group Size

   All members of an ongoing group.

Time Required

   One hour and forty minutes to two hours.

Materials

   I. One copy of a sheet of superlatives for each participant. Prior to conducting the activity, the facilitator prepares this sheet by referring to the following list; selecting as many superlatives as there are members in the group; and reproducing these superlatives on a sheet of paper, leaving a blank to the left of each so that a group member's name can be written in that space. (If the group consists of more than fourteen members, the facilitator should devise additional superlatives.)

     _____ Most friendly

     _____ Best worker

     _____ Most dependable

     _____ Most talented

     _____ Most group spirited

     _____ Best sport

     _____ Most deserving

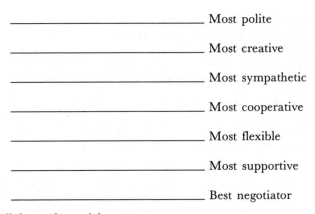

_____ Most polite

_____ Most creative

_____ Most sympathetic

_____ Most cooperative

_____ Most flexible

_____ Most supportive

_____ Best negotiator

II. A pencil for each participant.

III. A clipboard or other portable writing surface for each participant.

IV. A newsprint flip chart and a felt-tipped marker.

V. Masking tape for posting newsprint.

Physical Setting

Any room in which the group regularly meets. Chairs should be provided for the participants.

Process

I. The facilitator explains the goals of the activity and distributes copies of the sheet of superlatives and pencils.

II. The participants are asked to visualize a school yearbook that would portray the members of the immediate group. Each participant is instructed to work independently to fill in each blank on the sheet with the name of the one group member who best represents the superlative in question. The facilitator stipulates that each group member's name is to be written only once and that each participant should include himself or herself when considering whose name to write in each blank. While the participants are working, the facilitator reproduces the sheet of superlatives on newsprint and posts the newsprint. (Ten minutes.)

III. After all participants have completed the task, the participants take turns announcing their choices for the first superlative and their rationales for these choices. As the names are announced, the facilitator writes them on newsprint. The participants then discuss their choices until a consensus is reached regarding which group member most represents the superlative in question. The final choice is recorded on the original newsprint list in the blank to the left of that item. This procedure is followed until a consensus has been reached regarding each superlative. (Forty-five minutes.)

IV. The facilitator asks the participants to consider how the feedback given and received during the previous step has affected their perceptions of themselves and one another *in terms of their roles in the group.* The following questions may be useful during the ensuing discussion.

1. At this moment how do you feel about being a member of this group?
2. How do you feel about being assigned your particular superlative? How do you feel about any other superlatives for which you were nominated? How does your assigned superlative compare with the one you chose for yourself?
3. What positive contributions do you make to the group in your role as the superlative that you were assigned? What problems might your role cause within the group?
4. What have you learned about the way in which you are perceived by others?
5. Which other superlative would you like to have been assigned? What role would you like to develop in this group?
6. Who in the group was easy to assign to a superlative and why?
7. Who was difficult to assign and why?
8. What superlatives were missing to describe the members of your group?
9. What have you learned about your fellow group members?
10. How might you use what you have learned to help your group function better in the future?

(Thirty minutes.)

V. The facilitator assists the participants in turning the responses to the last question in Step IV into action steps that they can take to improve the group's functioning. These steps are recorded on newsprint and kept by the group so that the participants can refer to them from time to time.

Variations

I. Before beginning the activity, the facilitator may deliver a lecturette on giving and receiving feedback.

II. After Step IV the facilitator may lead a discussion on the evidence of risk taking during the activity and its effect on the group.

III. After Step V the facilitator may link what the participants have learned with a lecturette on group-member roles.

IV. After Step V the facilitator may conduct an activity that allows the participants to experiment with different roles.

Similar Structured Experiences: *Volume III:* Structured Experience **57;** *Vol. IV:* **104;** *'85 Annual:* **377;** *Vol. X:* **408.**

Lecturette Sources: *'72 Annual,* p. 197: "Openness, Collusion, and Feedback"; *'73 Annual,* p. 114: "The Johari Window: A Model for Soliciting and Giving Feedback."

Notes on the Use of "Yearbook":

Submitted by Bunty Ketcham and Alan Gilburg.

404. HEALTHY OR UNHEALTHY?: ASSESSING GROUP FUNCTIONING

Goals

I. To offer the participants an opportunity to assess the health of their group in terms of functional and dysfunctional member behaviors and to provide the group with feedback about this assessment.

II. To assist the participants in developing group definitions of a "healthy" group and an "unhealthy" group.

III. To help the participants to establish action steps to take to improve their group's functioning.

Group Size

All members of an intact group.

Time Required

Approximately two hours and fifteen minutes.

Materials

I. Several sheets of blank paper and a pencil for each participant.

II. A newsprint flip chart and a felt-tipped marker.

III. Masking tape for posting newsprint.

Physical Setting

A room in which the participants can work without being interrupted. Chairs and writing surfaces should be provided.

Process

I. The facilitator explains the goals of the activity.

II. Each participant is given several sheets of blank paper and a pencil and is asked to write the words "Healthy Group" and "Unhealthy Group" as two separate column headings on one of the sheets.

III. The facilitator instructs each participant to list under the appropriate heading at least three member behaviors that are characteristic of a healthy group and then to repeat this process for an unhealthy group. (Ten minutes.)

IV. All behaviors listed by the participants are elicited and transferred to separate newsprint lists of healthy-group characteristics and unhealthy-group characteristics. These lists are then posted prominently.

V. The facilitator leads a discussion about the listed behaviors, obtaining clarification of meaning as necessary. Then the facilitator assists the participants in achieving consensus regarding which behaviors should be included in each of the two lists. After consensus has been achieved, the facilitator writes the final lists on newsprint, posts these lists, and confirms with the participants that they accept the lists as definitions of a healthy group and an unhealthy group. (Thirty minutes.)

VI. Each participant is asked to indicate on another sheet of paper which behaviors from both definitions are typical of this group and whether he or she feels that the group is essentially healthy or unhealthy in terms of the agreed-on definitions. The facilitator instructs the participants not to put their names on their papers. (Ten minutes.)

VII. The facilitator collects all of the participants' papers. The behaviors listed on the papers are recorded on newsprint via tally marks. In addition, the participants' assessments of whether the group is healthy or unhealthy are recorded on newsprint via tally marks placed next to the appropriate list headings.

VIII. The facilitator leads a discussion of these results by asking the following questions:

1. What is your reaction to the results that have just been posted? How are you presently feeling about yourself as a member of this group? What else do you need to say at this time?

2. How accurately do these results represent your group? What dynamics do they seem to suggest?

3. What has this activity suggested to you about healthy and unhealthy group behavior in general? What "truths" about group effectiveness can be derived from what you have learned?

4. What may need to be changed about the definition of a healthy group and that of an unhealthy group?

5. What could you do to help your group to achieve greater health? How could a high degree of health be maintained by this group?

(Thirty minutes.)

Structured Experience 404

IX. Using the information elicited in the previous step, the facilitator assists the participants in determining action steps to take to correct the unhealthy behaviors identified and to improve the health of the group. The participants are encouraged to take notes during this process, to refer to these notes occasionally during the next few weeks to review the group's progress, and to bring the notes with them to a follow-up session to be held at a later date.

Variations

I. During Step IX a complete action plan with assigned responsibilities and monitoring procedures may be developed.

II. During Step VII, while the facilitator is recording the tally, the group members may be asked to list some behaviors that they could change and would be willing to change in the interest of group effectiveness. These behaviors are then shared during Step VIII.

Similar Structured Experiences: *Volume VIII:* Structured Experience **297**; *'82 Annual:* **326**.

Suggested Instruments: *'81 Annual,* p. 90: "Work-Group-Effectiveness Inventory"; *'83 Annual,* p. 103: "The Team Orientation and Behavior Inventory."

Lecturette Source: *'85 Annual,* p. 201: "Diagnosing and Changing Group Norms."

Notes on the Use of "Healthy or Unhealthy?":

Adapted from L. Thayer, "The Healthy Personality: Your Definition or Mine?," in L. Thayer (Ed.), *50 Strategies for Experiential Learning: Book Two,* University Associates, 1981.

405. STICKY WICKETS: EXPLORING GROUP STRESS

Goals

   I. To develop the participants' awareness of the factors that can lead to group stress.

   II. To allow the participants to experience some of these factors.

   III. To offer the participants an opportunity to share with one another their ideas for dealing with group stress.

Group Size

   Two or three intact groups.

Time Required

   One hour and forty-five minutes to two hours.

Materials

   I. A copy of the Sticky Wickets Discussion Sheet for each participant.

   II. A copy of the Sticky Wickets Group-Stress Theory Sheet for each participant.

   III. One sheet of blank paper and a pencil for each group's writer.

   IV. A newsprint flip chart and a felt-tipped marker.

Physical Setting

   A room that is slightly too small to accommodate group work so that each group experiences discomfort and distractions while completing its task. If the facilitator wishes, other environmental sources of stress may be added, such as loud music or an uncomfortable room temperature. A table and chairs for each group are optional; omitting them may add to group stress. However, if they are omitted, during Step VI the facilitator should provide each group's recorder with a clipboard or other portable writing surface.

Process

   I. The participants are instructed to assemble into their own groups.

II. The facilitator presents the task to be completed by each group:

"Your group is to prepare a report describing in detail all of the tasks that it performs. Start working now. No questions will be answered while you work on this report; you are expected to complete the task on your own."

III. After five minutes the facilitator makes the following comment:

"Each group is allowed to have only one member write its report. Decide now who that person is to be."

Each group's writer is given one sheet of blank paper and a pencil.

IV. After five more minutes the facilitator says, "Each group's report will be evaluated for neatness. Any group whose report is not neat will be penalized."

V. After three more minutes the facilitator comments as follows:

"You have fifteen minutes left in which to complete your work. Remember that each group's report will be evaluated."

As the participants work during the fifteen-minute period, the facilitator monitors their progress, occasionally commenting that the groups are not doing as well as expected.

VI. The facilitator calls time, collects the group reports, and gives each participant a copy of the Sticky Wickets Discussion Sheet. Each group is asked to discuss the questions on this sheet and to select one member to record the group's answers and to summarize these answers later in an oral presentation to the total group. (Thirty minutes.)

VII. The facilitator reassembles the total group and instructs the group recorders to take turns sharing their summaries. As the recorders present these summaries, the facilitator notes highlights and similarities among groups on newsprint. (Twenty minutes.)

VIII. Each participant is given a copy of the Sticky Wickets Group-Stress Theory Sheet and is asked to read this handout. (Ten minutes.)

IX. The facilitator leads a discussion in which the contents of the theory sheet are related to the activity just completed. The following questions are asked:

1. How would you characterize the level of *demands* associated with this task? the level of *constraints*? the level of *support*?
2. How does what happened in your group compare with the consequences identified by Payne?
3. Which group-member psychological state is most characteristic of your group: *deterioration, destruction,* or *development*?

4. What steps can your group take to deal more effectively with the sources of stress it encounters? Which sources of stress can be changed?
5. What will your changes accomplish?

Variations

I. After Step IX the participants may be asked to restructure the task to reduce the number and/or level of stress sources.

II. The task to be completed may be changed to reflect the composition of the groups involved. For example, when conducting the activity with intact managerial groups, the facilitator may ask each group to develop a new set of criteria and procedures for awarding promotions and salary increases.

III. Various factors cited in the theory sheet may be altered during task assignment and completion; for example, support may be provided, or the task difficulty may be increased or decreased.

Suggested Instruments: *'83 Annual,* p. 115: "Organizational Role Stress"; *'84 Annual,* p. 131: "Quality of Work Life-Conditions/Feelings (QWL-C/F)."
Lecturette Sources: *'81 Annual,* p. 138: "Stress-Management Skills: Self-Modification for Personal Adjustment to Stress"; *'83 Annual,* p. 170: "Stress, Communication, and Assertiveness: A Framework for Interpersonal Problem Solving."

Notes on the Use of "Sticky Wickets":

Submitted by William B. Kline and Joseph J. Blase.

STICKY WICKETS DISCUSSION SHEET

1. While your group was working on its report, how did you feel toward the facilitator?

2. How did you feel toward your fellow group members?

3. How did you feel about yourself?

4. How did the nature of the task itself and the way in which it was presented to you affect the preparation of the report?

5. What factors hindered your group in preparing its report?

6. What factors helped? In what ways were they helpful?

7. How consistent are your feelings about this task with those that you commonly experience as a member of this group? How common are the helping and hindering factors to your group?

STICKY WICKETS GROUP-STRESS THEORY SHEET

Literature in the field of stress management has proliferated in recent years. This body of literature has described numerous interventions that have proven to be effective in the prevention and management of stress that is experienced by individuals. More specifically, stress literature has focused on such topics as understanding sources of stress; individual responses to stress; cognitive coping strategies; diet; exercise; and such innovative approaches as meditation, hypnosis, and biofeedback. A survey of the stress literature demonstrates that the focus of the majority of investigations into the subject has been on how individuals can more effectively cope with stress.

An important aspect of stress that has been neglected until recently is the consideration of how various factors create stress for a group. Payne (1981) devised a model that depicts the phenomenon of task-group stress. This model is based on the notion that group process, environmental pressures, and the psychological states of members can result in destructive levels of group-experienced stress.

In the context of this model, "work" groups are those that have as their purpose the completing of specific tasks, such as producing products or making difficult decisions. The factors that determine a work group's experienced level of stress are *demands, constraints,* and *support.*

Demands

High levels of demands are likely to produce stress in a work group. Externally imposed demands related to the completion of tasks may include high degrees of task difficulty, high quality and/or quantity standards, and real or expected penalties for failing to meet these standards. Payne describes demands generated within the work group itself: the group's own standards for performance and rigid sanctions for "letting the group down" (for example, social isolation, blame, and so forth). Thus, a work group is likely to experience stress if it is subject to external demands, such as high quality and quantity standards, and internal demands, such as high performance and total commitment to the group's project.

Constraints

Constraints, the second factor presented by Payne, are defined as conditions that make it difficult or impossible for the work group to meet the demands placed on it. *Social constraints* are the outcome of behavioral, emotional, or cognitive factors operating on or in the work group. *Behavioral factors* that serve as constraints

---

R. Payne, "Stress in Task-Focused Groups," *Small Group Behavior,* Vol. 12, No. 3 (August 1981), pp. 253-268. Copyright © 1981 by Sage Publications, Inc. Adapted by permission of Sage Publications, Inc.

are normative standards such as rules, regulations, or other, more informal standards of behavior. For example, a work group may experience a behavioral constraint imposed by the organizational norm of not questioning authority. *Emotional factors* that constrain are the result of norms that govern the types of emotional expression considered appropriate. Should the expression of feelings of overwork, inadequacy, anxiety, or anger be regarded as inappropriate, it is likely that the group members' unexpressed feelings will contribute significantly to the intensity of stress experienced in the group. *Cognitive factors* that can constrain a work group are the beliefs that group members hold about the group. These beliefs may be that the group leader is ineffective, the group is incompetent, or successful task completion is impossible.

Physical or material constraints exist when a group works in surroundings that hinder its task completion, such as inadequate office space, or when a group has deficient or inadequate materials with which to complete its tasks, such as a parts shortage. *Time* also can be a significant constraint; insufficient time to complete even routine tasks can create substantial stress in a work group.

Support

Support is the final factor presented by Payne. A low level of support can cause stress in a work group. Support may include advice and consultation provided by superiors and colleagues, discussions among peers regarding feelings and frustrations, and steps taken by an organization to revise its regulations and procedures or to provide additional training.

Consequences of Work-Group Stress

Payne states that the group-stress variables interact to produce three classes of group-member psychological states: *deterioration, destruction,* and *development.* Low demands coupled with low levels of support and heavy constraints result in deterioration. For example, group members who perform repetitive, intellectually undemanding tasks under heavy or light behavioral constraints and with little or no support from one another may become apathetic or depressed. For people experiencing deterioration, work loses meaning and becomes a monotonous activity.

In situations in which demands are high, support is low, and constraints are either heavy or light, workers are likely to experience physically or psychologically destructive outcomes. Workers who function under high demands for quality and productivity and have little or no support in the work environment to assist in task completion, regardless of the constraints present, are likely to experience adverse psychological reactions such as burnout and/or physical reactions such as ulcers.

On the other hand, low or high demands, high levels of support, and light constraints produce a psychological state that leads to development. Work-group members who enjoy a high level of support from their families and one another and who face few constraining forces in their work environment are likely to be productive and to enjoy their work regardless of the level of demands imposed.

REFERENCE

Payne, R. Stress in task-focused groups. *Small Group Behavior,* 1981, *12,* 253-268.

406. AJAX APPLIANCE CORPORATION: EXPLORING CONFLICT-MANAGEMENT STYLES

Goals

    I. To illustrate various approaches to managing conflict and the ways in which these approaches affect the process of resolving a problem.

    II. To offer the participants opportunities to practice assigned approaches and to experiment with alternative approaches during role plays involving conflict.

Group Size

    Three or four groups of seven or eight participants each.

Time Required

    Two hours and twenty minutes.

Materials

    I. A copy of the Ajax Appliance Corporation Situation Sheet for each participant.

    II. A copy of the Ajax Appliance Corporation Theory Sheet for each participant.

    III. A set of Ajax Appliance Corporation Role Sheets A through F for each group (a different sheet for each of six members).

    IV. A copy of the Ajax Appliance Corporation Observer Sheet 1 for each observer.

    V. A copy of the Ajax Appliance Corporation Observer Sheet 2 for each observer.

    VI. A pencil for each observer.

    VII. A clipboard or other portable writing surface for each observer.

    VIII. Seven or eight name tags for each group. Prior to conducting the activity, the facilitator completes six of each group's tags with the job titles appearing on the role sheets and the remaining one or two tags with the word "Observer."

Physical Setting

A large room in which the groups can conduct their role plays without disturbing one another.

Process

I. The facilitator explains that the participants are to engage in a role play that focuses on conflict and problem resolution.

II. The participants are assembled into groups of seven or eight each. The facilitator distributes copies of the Ajax Appliance Corporation Situation Sheet and asks the participants to read this handout. (Five minutes.)

III. Role sheets are distributed within each group in such a way that each of six members receives a different sheet; each of the remaining members of the group receives a copy of the observer sheet, a pencil, and a clipboard or other portable writing surface. In addition, name tags are distributed within each group, and the participants are instructed to wear these tags for the duration of the activity.

IV. All participants are instructed to read their handouts, and the role players are asked to spend the next few minutes thinking about how to play their roles. During this time the facilitator instructs the observers in private in a separate area of the room, explaining that the role play is to be conducted in two phases and that a different observer sheet is to be filled out during each phase. (Ten minutes.)

V. The observers return to their groups. The facilitator clarifies the role-play situation as necessary, emphasizes the need for authentic role behavior to simulate reality, and instructs the groups to begin.

VI. After twenty minutes the facilitator stops the role plays, reassembles the total group, and asks the observers to share their observations. (Fifteen minutes.)

VII. The facilitator leads a discussion about the first phase of the activity by asking the following questions:

1. How did you feel about playing the role you were assigned? How did you feel about the behavior of the other role players?

2. How closely do your reactions during the role play resemble your typical reactions to conflict?

3. How would you describe each role player's approach to conflict?

4. What were the advantages of each approach? What were the disadvantages?

(Fifteen minutes.)

VIII. Each participant is given a copy of the Ajax Appliance Corporation Theory Sheet and is asked to read this sheet. The facilitator leads a brief discussion about the content of the sheet, relating it to the first phase of the activity. (Twenty minutes.)

IX. The participants are instructed to return to their groups and to begin their role plays again, but with the following difference: Each role player is to try a different conflict-management approach with which he or she would like to experiment, and the role players are not to announce what these new approaches will be. Each observer is given a copy of observer sheet 2 and is instructed to answer the questions on this sheet.

X. After twenty minutes the role plays are stopped, the total group is reconvened, and the observers are instructed to share their observations. (Fifteen minutes.)

XI. The facilitator leads a concluding discussion. The following questions are asked:

1. Which conflict-management approach did you try this time? How did this approach feel to you? What different reactions did you experience?

2. In what ways did your new approach to conflict work better or worse than the approach that you were assigned originally? How did this approach work with the approaches that the others chose?

3. How can you account for any differences between the first and second role plays? What do these differences suggest to you?

4. What can you conclude about the different conflict-handling approaches? How do your conclusions compare with what the theory sheet suggests? How do they compare with your own experiences with conflict in an organizational setting?

5. How might you deal with conflict differently in the future? What changes are you willing to try?

Variations

I. The theory sheet may be presented at the end of the activity so that the participants can choose alternative conflict approaches for the second role play without the benefit of the theory.

II. An "ideal" role play of the situation concentrating on resolution may be enacted and discussed in terms of the theory.

III. Each group may be assigned a different conflict-management approach, with all role players exhibiting behaviors consistent with the one approach assigned their particular group. The results are then compared and contrasted in a total-group discussion.

IV. If a large number of participants are involved, the facilitator may assemble six large groups. Each group is assigned a different role, selects one member to play that role, and coaches that member about how to behave during Step VI. After the theory sheet has been distributed, each group coaches its role player about how to behave in order to achieve resolution in a second role play. During each of the role plays, the participant coaches act as observers.

Similar Structured Experiences: *'78 Annual:* Structured Experience **224;** *'82 Annual:* **323.**

Suggested Instruments: *'81 Annual,* p. 100: "Diagnosing Organizational Conflict-Management Climates"; *'82 Annual,* p. 83: "Conflict-Management Style Survey."

Lecturette Sources: *'73 Annual,* p. 135: "Confrontation: Types, Conditions, and Outcomes"; *'74 Annual,* p. 139: "Conflict-Resolution Strategies"; *'77 Annual,* p. 115: "Constructive Conflict in Discussions: Learning To Manage Disagreements Effectively," p. 120: "Handling Group and Organizational Conflict"; *'82 Annual,* p. 135: "Coping with Conflict."

Notes on the Use of "Ajax Appliance Corporation":

Submitted by Judith L. Grewell, Michael L. Gracey, Geraldine Platt, and Dale N. DeHaven.

Structured Experience 406

AJAX APPLIANCE CORPORATION SITUATION SHEET

You are an employee of the Ajax Appliance Corporation, which manufactures washing machines. For some time now, the company has been suffering because the quality of its products is deteriorating. Recently *Consumer Reports* listed Ajax's top-of-the-line washing machine as "unreliable and breakdown prone." Even some of the appliance stores in your own town, which is the home of Ajax's main office, have canceled their contracts to carry Ajax products.

A year ago the problem was diagnosed as resulting from inefficiency in the production process. Since that time five consultants specializing in correcting efficiency problems have been retained by the company, but not one of them has been able to help. Three weeks ago Ajax hired a full-time industrial engineer to work solely on this problem. The top management at Ajax has given this engineer six months to correct the inefficiency in production and upgrade the quality of Ajax's products. If no improvement has been made in six months, the company will close its doors permanently.

The industrial engineer has just called a meeting of key production personnel to discuss how best to approach the task. You are on your way to the meeting now.

AJAX APPLIANCE CORPORATION THEORY SHEET

Five different styles of managing conflict were identified by Thomas and Kilmann (1974):

1. *Competition* indicates a desire to meet one's own needs and a lack of concern for the needs of the other people involved in the conflict. In employing this style, the competitor uses some form of power, which may be connected with his or her position, rank, expertise, or ability to persuade or coerce.

2. *Collaboration* reflects a desire to meet the needs of all people involved in the conflict, not just one's own needs. The collaborator is highly assertive, as is the competitor; but, unlike the competitor, the collaborator cooperates with everyone involved so that all needs are acknowledged as important, alternative resolutions and their consequences are identified, and the alternative that meets each person's goals is chosen and implemented.

3. *Avoidance* reflects a desire to evade the matter at hand. The individual who uses this style does not demonstrate a strong concern for anyone's needs, including his or her own. This approach is neither assertive nor cooperative.

4. *Accommodation* indicates a willingness to meet the needs of the other people involved at the expense of one's own needs. Cooperation is the primary behavior manifested with this style; unlike the competitor and the collaborator, the individual who accommodates does not behave assertively.

5. *Compromise* reflects a desire to find a resolution that will partially meet the needs of everyone involved. The individual who approaches conflict with compromise in mind expects the outcome to be mutually acceptable and somewhat satisfying to all of the parties; he or she also expects to give up something in order to achieve a resolution that everyone can live with. This style is both assertive and cooperative, but to a lesser degree than is collaboration.

Adapted from M.B. Ross, "Coping with Conflict," in J.W. Pfeiffer and L.D. Goodstein (Eds.), *The 1982 Annual for Facilitators, Trainers, and Consultants,* University Associates, 1982.

Structured Experience 406

Each of these styles is appropriate under certain circumstances. Although each of us tends to use one or more particular styles more often than the others, all of us can learn to use all five and can benefit from the availability of a wide range of behaviors in conflict situations.

REFERENCE

Thomas, K.W., & Kilmann, R.H. *Thomas-Kilmann Conflict Mode Instrument.* Tuxedo, NY: XICOM, 1974.

AJAX APPLIANCE CORPORATION ROLE SHEET A

Industrial Engineer

You were just graduated from college, and this is your first full-time job. You know that Ajax's problem is serious, but you have done a lot of research on the subject of plant efficiency and are sure that you have the solution. When you studied Ajax's plant layout, you realized that it was hopelessly outdated; consequently, you have spent the last two weeks designing a new layout that will eliminate two work stations, save money for Ajax, and streamline the entire operation. You are extremely pleased with your work on this project and you are looking forward to telling the key production personnel about your plan. Although the new layout means that two people will have to be laid off, you are sure that you can convince those attending the meeting that this move will pay off in the long run.

You know that a lot is at stake during this meeting, not just for Ajax but for you as well. If the implementation of the new plant layout succeeds in increasing efficiency and product quality is enhanced—and you are sure that this will be the case—you will be in an excellent position for a promotion. Therefore, you intend to have your way during the meeting, no matter what.

Do not show this role description to anyone.

AJAX APPLIANCE CORPORATION ROLE SHEET B

Plant Manager

You have been an Ajax employee for twenty-three years. You started on the production line and have worked your way up to your present position. You are absolutely convinced that the problems Ajax is experiencing at the moment are attributable to its outmoded production equipment; you personally know all of the plant workers, and they are first rate, but they are struggling to operate old equipment that breaks down frequently and causes them to lose valuable production time. You consider yourself to be an advocate for these workers, and your plan for this meeting is to obtain a commitment from the new industrial engineer to buy the new equipment that is so desperately needed.

You are determined to have your way during the meeting. The plant workers are counting on you, and you refuse to let them down.

Do not show this role description to anyone.

Structured Experience   406

AJAX APPLIANCE CORPORATION ROLE SHEET C

Production Supervisor, First Shift

You have been with Ajax for nine years now. You like your job and you want to keep it. Like most other Ajax employees, you are concerned about the inefficiency in production that seems to have led to lower product quality, but you have been unable to figure out a solution to the problem. You are hoping that it will simply correct itself in time. You do not believe that discussing the situation in the upcoming meeting will do any good. In fact, you are afraid that tempers will flare, and just the thought of conflict makes you extremely uncomfortable.

You plan to keep a low profile during the meeting, to refrain from voicing any opinions unless directly asked, and to avoid taking sides for or against anyone present. The last thing you intend to do is to "rock the boat."

Do not show this role description to anyone.

AJAX APPLIANCE CORPORATION ROLE SHEET D

Production Supervisor, Second Shift

You have been an Ajax employee for five years. You are very worried about the current inefficiency in production that has led to quality problems. You feel that the source of the problem is twofold: (1) an outdated plant layout that includes unnecessary steps in the production process, and (2) outdated plant equipment that breaks down frequently, making it difficult to meet production deadlines and causing tremendous headaches for the production workers.

You have talked extensively with your subordinates and have spent a great deal of time observing them as they work, and you are convinced that the majority of them are hard workers who are just as concerned about Ajax's present situation as you are. However, you do know of one employee on your shift whose attitude is not what it should be, and you have been thinking about laying off this person; without him, perhaps the shift morale and productivity would improve. You have been meaning to discuss this employee with the plant manager, but the manager is so loyal to the workers that you feel a proposed layoff will be met with resistance; however, you have made up your mind that you will bring up the idea at today's meeting. If your proposal is, in fact, met with resistance, you plan to tell the manager that you would be willing *not* to lay off this employee if the manager would support a new plant layout as well as new equipment.

Do not show this role description to anyone.

AJAX APPLIANCE CORPORATION ROLE SHEET E

Production Supervisor, Third Shift

You have been with Ajax for six months. In the past few weeks you have been hearing rumors that the company will shut down if the inefficiency in production is not corrected, and these rumors frighten you. Before you were hired at Ajax, you were out of work for a year; during that time you and your family suffered greatly, and you do not care to repeat that experience. Today's meeting worries you in terms of its possible ramifications. You are fairly certain from what you have observed that the inefficiency lies with the plant layout, which is terribly outdated. It has occurred to you that at least one work station could be eliminated, and you feel that you must state your observation and opinion during the meeting. However, you know that the plant manager, who is powerful at Ajax and considered to be an advocate for the production workers, probably will not take kindly to your idea of eliminating one or more work stations because this approach would mean a loss of jobs for the people who work at these stations.

Stating how you feel about the situation is as far as you will go during the meeting. If you meet with resistance from the plant manager, you will yield to the manager's point of view; you cannot risk jeopardizing your job and your family's future.

Do not show this role description to anyone.

AJAX APPLIANCE CORPORATION ROLE SHEET F

Assistant Plant Manager

Although you have been with Ajax for only a year, you feel a strong commitment to the company. You are concerned about the inefficiency in production, but you believe in the company's ability to find a solution and to survive.

Like the plant manager, you believe that the problem is attributable to outmoded production equipment; unlike the manager, however, you are willing to listen to other ideas on the subject. During the upcoming meeting you want to make sure that the goals of everyone present are heard and that the group chooses a solution that incorporates all of these goals. You realize that finding such a solution will not be easy, but you feel that saving Ajax through this approach will lead to a healthier, happier company in the long run.

Do not show this role description to anyone.

AJAX APPLIANCE CORPORATION OBSERVER SHEET 1

Instructions: During the upcoming role play, you are to observe the interactions of your fellow group members and to write answers to the following questions. Later you will be asked to share your questions and answers with the total group.

1. What behaviors do you observe on the part of each role player as the Ajax situation is being discussed?

2. How do individuals react to the different behaviors?

3. What effect does each type of behavior have on the group process?

4. What is the effect of each on moving the group toward a decision?

AJAX APPLIANCE CORPORATION OBSERVER SHEET 2

Instructions: During the second role play, you are to observe again the interactions of the role players and to write answers to the following questions. Later you will again be asked to share your questions and answers with the total group.

1. What differences are you observing between this role play and the previous one?

2. What conflict-handling approaches do the individual role players seem to be using?

3. How are people reacting differently to these different approaches?

4. What effect are the different approaches having on the group process?

5. What is the effect of each on moving the group toward a decision?

407. THE VALUE PROFILE: LEGITIMIZING INTERGROUP DIFFERENCES

Goals

    I. To help two work groups within an organization to understand and accept the legitimacy of each other's values so that they can interact more effectively.

    II. To assist each group in establishing its own profile of values.

Group Size

    All members of two intact work groups.

Time Required

    One hour and forty-five minutes to two hours.

Materials

    I. A copy of The Value Profile Work Sheet for each participant.

    II. A newsprint flip chart and a felt-tipped marker.

Physical Setting

    A room large enough to accommodate a group-on-group configuration.[1] Movable chairs should be provided for the participants.

Process

    I. The facilitator introduces the goals of the activity.

    II. The participants are asked to assemble into a group-on-group configuration.

    III. Each participant is given a copy of The Value Profile Work Sheet and is asked to read the instructions on this sheet. The facilitator explains that

---

[1]A group-on-group configuration consists of two groups of participants: One group forms a circle and actively participates in an activity; the other group forms a circle around the first group and observes the first group's activity.

the members of the group in the inner circle are to engage in the first discussion and establish their group profile; the members of the group in the outer circle are to listen to, but not participate in, this discussion.

IV. The participants in the inner circle are instructed to begin; the facilitator assists them as necessary during the value-clarification procedure and records their preferred terms on newsprint. At the conclusion of the discussion, the facilitator reviews the group's profile and confirms that all members accept the recorded terms as group values. (Thirty minutes.)

V. The two groups exchange circles, and Step IV is repeated. (Thirty minutes.)

VI. The facilitator posts the two newsprint lists of terms side by side. The participants are instructed to move their chairs as necessary so that they can see both lists. The facilitator then leads a discussion of the activity, emphasizing the legitimacy of both sets of values. The following questions are asked:

1. What reactions did you have to discussing your group's values? What were your reactions while listening to the other group's values?

2. What happened in your group while establishing the profile? What happened in the other group? How did the development of the group discussions fit with the value profiles that were established?

3. What new insights do you have about your own group? What insights have you gained about the other group?

4. What can you conclude about group values in general?

5. How can you legitimize group values that are different from those of your own group?

6. What can you do to increase understanding and acceptance between these two groups? How can you demonstrate your understanding and acceptance?

7. How will your new understandings create more effective work relationships between these two groups?

Variations

I. Prior to each group-on-group discussion, the members of the observer group may be given pencils and observer sheets and asked to take notes about their observations.

II. After each of the group-on-group discussions, the members of the observer group may be asked to demonstrate their understanding of the inside group's value profile, to ask questions for the purpose of clarification, and/or to voice agreements or disagreements.

III. The participants may be asked to complete the work sheet individually before the group-on-group discussions.

IV. The facilitator may arrange a follow-up session with the participants to track change and progress.

Suggested Instrument: *'85 Annual,* p. 107: "The Personal Value Statement (PVS): An Experiential Learning Instrument."

Lecturette Sources: *'73 Annual,* p. 135: "Confrontation: Types, Conditions, and Outcomes"; *'74 Annual,* p. 139: "Conflict-Resolution Strategies"; *'77 Annual,* p. 115: "Constructive Conflict in Discussions: Learning To Manage Disagreements Effectively," p. 120: "Handling Group and Organizational Conflict"; *'85 Annual,* p. 169: "A Taxonomy of Intergroup Conflict-Resolution Strategies."

Notes on the Use of "The Value Profile":

Submitted by Edward F. Pajak.

THE VALUE PROFILE WORK SHEET

Instructions: You and your fellow group members are to work toward establishing a group value profile. To accomplish this goal, you will be discussing each of the following pairs of terms separately and deciding which of the two terms represents a value that your group holds. During the discussion you should consider such factors as your work styles, the kinds of tasks you perform, and your attitudes toward your work.

belonging	individuality
risk	safety
natural	rational
status	achievement
cooperation	competition
change	stability
loyalty	opportunity
facts	feelings
flexible	dependable
formal	informal

408. KALEIDOSCOPE:
TEAM BUILDING THROUGH ROLE EXPANSION

Goals

I. To allow members of a team to clarify their roles and to give and receive feedback about their existing and potential contributions to the team.

II. To promote team building through self-disclosure, feedback, and commitment among team members.

III. To widen the team members' views of one another's abilities and valuable qualities.

Group Size

All members of an intact work group.

Time Required

Two hours and twenty minutes to approximately six hours. (The time required varies according to group size. A group of four can complete the activity in approximately three hours, but a group of ten requires approximately six hours. A group with more than ten members should be accommodated in two sessions, with all members attending each session. See Step III for time required *per team member*.)

Materials

I. A copy of the Kaleidoscope Work Sheet for each team member.

II. A pencil for each team member.

III. A clipboard or other portable writing surface for each team member.

Physical Setting

A room with chairs arranged in a circle so that the team members can see one another during the activity.

Process

I. The facilitator explains the goals of the activity.

II. Each team member is given a copy of the Kaleidoscope Work Sheet, a pencil, and a clipboard or other portable writing surface and is asked to complete the work sheet. The facilitator provides the following examples of abilities and/or qualities that are assets in jobs:

1. A medical researcher might state that he or she *is detail oriented* and *has an ability to organize data effectively;* and

2. A screenwriter might state that he or she *has a lively imagination* and *an ability to write realistic dialog.*

(Twenty minutes.)

III. After all team members have completed their work sheets, they are asked to take turns sharing the contents of these sheets. The facilitator explains the procedure as follows:

1. While one member is sharing, the rest of the team listens carefully.

2. After the member reads his or her response to Item 1 on the work sheet, the other team members ask for any necessary clarification and state any reactions that might be useful as feedback.

3. This procedure is followed until all six items have been reviewed and the other team members have expressed whatever commitments they are willing to make regarding Item 6. In addition, when providing feedback concerning the content of Items 1 and 2, the other team members suggest any abilities and/or qualities that have not been listed.

The facilitator encourages each member to take notes while he or she is receiving feedback. (Thirty minutes *per team member.*)

IV. The facilitator leads a concluding discussion by asking the following questions:

1. What was your reaction to sharing your used strengths, your unused strengths, and your ideal picture of your job?

2. How do you feel about your chances for turning your ideal picture of your job into reality?

3. How can you evaluate your own progress toward realizing your ideal picture of your job?

4. What did you learn about yourself as a member of this team?

5. What did you learn about your fellow members?

6. How might this activity affect your future relationships with your fellow members?

7. How can the entire team evaluate the impact of this activity?

(Twenty minutes.)

Structured Experience   408

V. Each team member is instructed to keep his or her work sheet to refer to from time to time and to bring to a follow-up session to be held in a few months. The facilitator states that during this session progress will be discussed and other plans and commitments may be made.

Variations

I. The facilitator may begin the activity with the presentation and discussion of a visual aid depicting each member's current role and the interrelationship of the various roles.

II. After Step IV the team members may engage in a contracting activity, planning to take some steps toward the ideal before the group next meets.

III. After Step IV the team members may work individually to transform their wishes and their fellow members' feedback into written job descriptions, which could then be used at the follow-up session.

Similar Structured Experiences: *Volume III:* Structured Experience **57;** *Vol. IV:* **104;** *Vol. V:* **171;** *'85 Annual:* **386;** *Vol. X:* **403.**

Suggested Instrument: *'85 Annual,* p. 101: "The Team Effectiveness Critique."

Lecturette Source: *'80 Annual,* p. 152: "Job-Related Adaptive Skills: Toward Personal Growth."

Notes on the Use of "Kaleidoscope":

Submitted by Carlo E. Cetti and Mary Kirkpatrick Craig.

KALEIDOSCOPE WORK SHEET

1. List two abilities and/or qualities that you possess that are assets to you in your present job.

2. List two valuable abilities and/or qualities that you possess but are currently not using in your job.

3. What is your ideal picture of your job and your role in this team? How would this ideal incorporate your unused abilities and/or qualities?

4. What positive contributions could you make to this team by actualizing some of the aspects of your ideal picture of your job?

5. What aspects of your ideal picture of your job can you turn into reality? What specific steps can you take? What might help you as you try to take these steps? What might hinder you?

6. How can your fellow team members help you to capitalize on your strengths and to actualize at least some parts of your ideal picture?

409. SHARING PERSPECTIVES: EXCHANGING VIEWS ON MANAGERIAL AND WORKER ATTITUDES

Goals

I. To explore the origins of certain managerial and worker attitudes.

II. To allow the participants to share and discuss their personal feelings about these attitudes.

III. To help a manager and his or her subordinates to develop a greater understanding of one another so that their relationships can be improved in the future.

Group Size

All members of an intact work group, including the manager. This activity requires that the participants have previous training in trust building.

Time Required

Approximately two hours.

Materials

I. A copy of the Sharing Perspectives Manager Sheet for the manager.

II. A copy of the Sharing Perspectives Worker Sheet for each subordinate.

III. A pencil for each participant.

IV. Newsprint and a felt-tipped marker.

V. Newsprint reproductions of the manager sheet and the worker sheet. The facilitator should prepare these reproductions prior to conducting the activity.

VI. Masking tape for posting newsprint.

Physical Setting

A room with movable chairs for the participants.

Process

I. The facilitator introduces the goals of the activity.

II. The manager is given a copy of the Sharing Perspectives Manager Sheet and a pencil, and each subordinate is given a copy of the Sharing Perspectives Worker Sheet and a pencil. The participants are asked to complete their sheets. (Ten minutes.)

III. While the participants are working, the facilitator writes the following questions on newsprint:

1. What is really meant by the statement?
2. What might have created the attitude behind it?
3. Why do you consider it true or false?

IV. The facilitator posts a newsprint copy of the manager sheet. The manager is instructed to join the facilitator in the center of the room, and the subordinates are asked to form a circle around their manager and the facilitator. The manager is instructed to share his or her responses to each statement on the manager sheet and to discuss each statement with the facilitator in terms of the three questions listed on newsprint. The subordinates are asked to listen and observe while their manager and the facilitator engage in this discussion. (Fifteen minutes.)

V. A newsprint copy of the worker sheet is posted. The subordinates are asked to join the facilitator in a circle in the center of the room, and the manager is instructed to be seated outside this circle. The workers are asked to share their responses to each statement on their handout and to discuss each statement in terms of the same three newsprint questions. The manager is instructed to listen and observe while the facilitator and the subordinates engage in this discussion. (One hour.)

VI. The manager is invited to rejoin the group. The facilitator assists the manager and the subordinates in establishing a dialog so that questions and concerns about the preceding discussions may be addressed. (Ten minutes.)

VII. The facilitator leads the total group in a discussion of the activity. The following questions are asked:

1. When you were observing, how did you react to the assumption that people in your position make the kinds of statements that were listed on newsprint?

2. What parts of the discussion you observed were particularly interesting, meaningful, or surprising to you?
3. How did you feel as you discussed your sheet? What might account for your feelings?
4. What dynamics between you and your manager or you and your subordinates can be explained by this experience? What happened during the discussions that shed light on those dynamics?
5. What conclusions can you draw about manager and worker perceptions? What do you understand better about these perceptions?
6. How might your perceptions of your manager or subordinates change as a result of this activity? What kinds of behavioral changes might your new perceptions result in? How might you treat one another differently?

Variations

I. If the worker group is particularly large or if the facilitator wishes to shorten the time allotted for Steps IV and V, the manager and worker sheets may be shortened to five statements each.

II. The facilitator may devise different manager and worker sheets based on predetermined problems that are unique to the work group involved.

III. After Step VII the participants may be instructed to develop specific action plans to address the issues of concern that were uncovered during the activity.

IV. A follow-up session may be planned to reinforce any positive changes.

V. The activity may be conducted with two or three intact work groups within an organization, including their managers.

Similar Structured Experience: *'81 Annual:* Structured Experience **289.**
Suggested Instruments: *'76 Annual,* p. 101: "Organization Behavior Describer Survey (OBDS)"; *'78 Annual,* p. 81: "Organizational Norms Opinionnaire"; *Vol. VIII,* p. 13: "People on the Job Work Sheet."

Adapted from G. Silverman, "Racial Awareness: A Black-White Communications Experience," in H. L. Fromkin and J. J. Sherwood (Eds.), *Intergroup and Minority Relations: An Experiential Handbook,* University Associates, 1976.

Notes on the Use of "Sharing Perspectives":

SHARING PERSPECTIVES MANAGER SHEET

Instructions: Imagine that each of the following statements is made to you by one of your subordinates. Designate whether you find each statement true or false by placing a check mark in the appropriate column.

Worker Statement	True	False
1. "Managers never have enough time for their subordinates."		
2. "Managers think and act exactly the way their superiors tell them to."		
3. "Managers don't care what their subordinates think or want or how their subordinates feel."		
4. "Managers have no idea what it's like to be one of the workers in an organization."		
5. "The most important thing to managers is getting ahead."		
6. "The ones who do the real work in organizations are the workers, not the managers."		
7. "Managers always act superior; they don't realize how competent their subordinates are."		
8. "The only time a manager talks to subordinates is when they've done something wrong."		
9. "Managers take the credit for their subordinates' good work."		
10. "Managers tell their subordinates to do things without knowing what's really going on."		

SHARING PERSPECTIVES WORKER SHEET

Instructions: Imagine that each of the following statements is made to you by your manager. Designate whether you find each statement true or false by placing a check mark in the appropriate column.

Manager Statement	True	False
1. "Workers are only interested in collecting their paychecks."		
2. "It's not a manager's job to motivate subordinates; workers should be self-motivated."		
3. "Workers aren't willing to make sacrifices for the organization."		
4. "Workers are clock watchers who will shirk their duties if they're not watched constantly."		
5. "Workers want to be spoon-fed; they always expect their managers to solve their problems."		
6. "Workers have no real respect for their managers."		
7. "Every worker thinks that his or her job is the most important in the organization."		
8. "Workers fail to see the importance of team efforts."		
9. "Workers aren't concerned with the profitability of the organization."		
10. "Workers never tell their managers what's really going on."		

410. THE PEOPLE OF TRION: EXPLORING ORGANIZATIONAL VALUES

Goals

I. To offer the participants an opportunity to examine their organizational values.

II. To explore the implications of the participants' organizational values.

III. To explore the implications of differences between personal and organizational values.

IV. To examine the ways in which people are taught organizational values.

Group Size

Two or three groups of eight to ten participants each.

Time Required

Approximately two hours.

Materials

I. A copy of The People of Trion Role Sheet A for each participant Trionian.

II. A copy of The People of Trion Role Sheet B for each participant businessperson and each observer.

III. A copy of The People of Trion Observer Sheet for each observer.

IV. Blank paper and a pencil for each participant.

Physical Setting

A main assembly room in which each group can conduct its role play and discussions without disturbing the other group(s). A table and chairs should be provided for each group. In addition, a separate room with a table and chairs should be provided for the use of the participant Trionians in preparing to play their roles.

Process

I. The facilitator explains the goals of the activity.

II. The participants are assembled into groups of eight to ten participants each, and each group is seated at a separate table. The facilitator distributes handouts and supplies to each group: Three participants receive role sheet A; four participants receive role sheet B; and the remaining participants receive the observer sheet as well as role sheet B. In addition, each participant is given blank paper and a pencil. Then all participants are instructed to read their handouts. (Ten minutes.)

III. The participants who are to play the Trionians are asked to leave the main assembly room and to be seated at a table in a separate room. The groups of businesspeople and observers are instructed to spend the next few minutes thinking and making notes about how to proceed with their tasks. The facilitator leaves the room to join the Trionians, elicits and answers questions about what they are to do when the individual group role plays commence, and emphasizes the importance of maintaining their roles during the role plays. Then the Trionians are instructed to spend the next thirty minutes discussing among themselves how to approach the playing of their roles and making notes about questions that they would like to ask the businesspeople.

IV. The facilitator returns to the main assembly room, elicits and answers questions from the various groups of businesspeople about what they are to do during the role plays, and instructs these groups to begin their meetings in preparation for educating the Trionians. The facilitator also emphasizes how important it is for the businesspeople to be sensitive to the background and the needs of the Trionians as they plan their approach and during the upcoming role plays.

V. After the businesspeople have completed their plans, the facilitator invites the Trionians to return to the main assembly room and to rejoin their original groups. Then the businesspeople are instructed to begin the individual group role plays with the Trionians.

VI. After thirty minutes the facilitator tells the participants to stop their role plays. The observers are instructed to share and discuss their questions and answers about both phases of the activity with their fellow group members, and the businesspeople and Trionians are instructed to share and discuss the difficulties they experienced in playing their roles. (Thirty minutes.)

VII. The facilitator reassembles the total group for a concluding discussion during which the following questions are asked:

1. What questions were raised in your mind about the values expressed in American organizations? How did you react to those questions? What do your questions and reactions say about your values?
2. What does this role play symbolize about the ways in which we teach and learn organizational values? How does the teaching process used during the role play compare with the process used in your organization?
3. What statements seem to be true about American organizational values?
4. How have you felt in the past when your personal values conflicted with your organization's values?
5. If you were to replay your role now, what would you do differently?
6. What might you do differently in your organization in the future with regard to acting out your personal values? What might you do differently when reacting to the organization's values?

Variations

I. Participants may be assigned to observe the Trionians' discussion in Step III.

II. After Step VII the groups may be asked to conduct their role plays again, based on the total-group discussion and what they have learned.

III. The role of the businesspeople may be changed to that of representatives from another institution, such as government or education.

IV. The role of the Trionians may be changed to that of members of a warlike society.

V. The goals of the activity may be refocused to the process of education and/or training, and the total-group discussion may concentrate on adaptation to minorities, different ethnic backgrounds, and so forth.

Similar Structured Experience: *'83 Annual:* Structured Experience **339.**
Suggested Instruments: *'75 Annual,* p. 101: "Diagnosing Organizational Ideology"; *'78 Annual,* p. 81: "Organizational Norms Opinionnaire."
Lecturette Sources: *'75 Annual,* p. 199: "Understanding Your Organization's Character"; *'77 Annual,* p. 123: "Organizational Norms."

Submitted by B.J. Allen, Jr.

Notes on the Use of "The People of Trion":

THE PEOPLE OF TRION ROLE SHEET A

Native Trionian

You are a native of Trion, a primitive society deep within the interior of Brazil. Recently Trion was threatened by an invading tribe, and the government of the United States came to its rescue. You and almost all of your fellow Trionians were successfully airlifted to the United States. You have been in this country for a number of months now and have been taught English and provided with food, clothing, and shelter.

Trion was a simple society with a primitive technology. Its agrarian economy provided the basic needs of life, and each Trionian labored toward the production of these necessities. Governance in Trion was by consensus of the members of the Trionate, a body of citizens whose membership rotated every six months. Each adult Trionian was expected to serve one, and only one, term as a member of the Trionate.

Few social institutions existed in Trion; marriage and formal religion, for example, were unknown. People fell in love, lived together, and reared their children. Trionians were and are of the highest moral character. Violence was rare in Trion, though minor violations were occasionally committed against an individual or the community. In all such cases, the punishment, which was determined by a sub-committee of the Trionate, consisted of isolation for varying periods of time.

Competition did not exist in Trion; neither did businesses. Consequently, the whole language of corporate America is strange to you and your fellow Trionians. Although you have found Americans to be kind and generous, their habits, life styles, and ideas about working continue to confuse you. Now you have been told that you and the other Trionians are to meet with a group of representative American businesspeople, who will teach you what you need to know in order to enter and succeed in the American job market. You are looking forward to this meeting because you are certain that the businesspeople will help you to understand the ways of the American people.

THE PEOPLE OF TRION ROLE SHEET B

American Businessperson

You have been chosen to be a member of a team of experts on the way in which American organizations operate. Your team's task is to explain to some people from Trion, a primitive society deep within the interior of Brazil, how the American concept of work is carried out in organizations. A number of months ago Trion was threatened by an invading tribe, and the government of the United States came to its rescue. Almost all Trionians were successfully airlifted to the United States; provided with food, clothing, and shelter; and taught English. Now these people are ready to take the next step toward becoming integrated into American society: They are about to enter the job market. You and your fellow team members are to educate these people about what they can expect with regard to life in American organizations, what opportunities exist within such organizations, and what pitfalls to avoid. Here are some terms that you might want to consider defining during the course of your explanation:

job interview	work team
worker	productivity
supervisor/boss	meetings
manager	schedules
CEO	deadlines
behavioral standards	motivation
organizational norms/values	incentives (e.g., raises, promotions)
time card	performance review
salary	termination
job description	corporation
responsibilities	competition
goal setting	profit and loss

You need not cover all of these terms and you need not feel restricted to only the terms listed. Consider the list as a starting point. In a few minutes you will be meeting with the other members of your team to discuss an approach to take in educating the Trionians.

The copy that follows consists of background information about the people of Trion. This information should help you in determining what to say to these people.

The Trionians

Trion was a simple society with a primitive technology. Its agrarian economy provided the basic needs of life, and each Trionian labored toward the production of these necessities. Governance in Trion was by consensus of the members of the Trionate, a body of citizens whose membership rotated every six months. Each adult Trionian was expected to serve one, and only one, term as a member of the Trionate.

Few social institutions existed in Trion; marriage and formal religion, for example, were unknown. People fell in love, lived together, and reared their children. Trionians were and are of the highest moral character. Violence was rare in Trion, though minor violations were occasionally committed against an individual or the community. In all such cases, the punishment, which was determined by a subcommittee of the Trionate, consisted of isolation for varying periods of time.

Competition did not exist in Trion; neither did businesses. Consequently, the whole language of corporate America is strange to the Trionians. Americans' habits, life styles, and ideas about working continue to confuse them. It is hoped that you and your fellow team members will demonstrate a high degree of concern and caring as you help these people to develop an understanding of life in American organizations.

THE PEOPLE OF TRION OBSERVER SHEET

Instructions: Your task is twofold: (1) to observe a group of American businesspeople as they discuss an approach to take in educating the Trionians, and (2) to observe the interactions of these businesspeople and the Trionians during the ensuing educational session. Read the content of role sheet B so that you will be familiar with the task assigned to the businesspeople as well as the situation of the Trionians.

As you observe these two phases of the activity, write the answers to the following questions. Do not enter into any conversations with the businesspeople or the Trionians. Later you will be asked to share your observations with the group to which you have been assigned.

Phase 1: The Meeting of the Businesspeople

1. What terms are the businesspeople choosing to define? How are they defining these terms?

2. What issues are raised as the businesspeople approach the task? What are the areas of agreement? What are the areas of disagreement?

3. What do their choice of terms, their definitions, and their explanation of organizational life say about the organizational values these people hold?

4. Are the businesspeople more concerned with the people of Trion or with their own explanation of organizational life? What does their focus suggest about organizational values?

5. How are the businesspeople acting out their organizational values as they conduct the meeting?

Phase 2: The Meeting of the Businesspeople with the Trionians

1. How are the businesspeople approaching the Trionians? What choices are they making in presenting their explanation? What changes, if any, are they making in their original plan?

2. How do you account for the approach being taken?

3. What *explicit* values are the businesspeople emphasizing? What *implicit* values are they emphasizing?

4. How are the Trionians reacting to the explanation?

5. What major questions are the Trionians asking? What values do these questions imply? How are these questions being treated by the businesspeople?

6. What differences in values between the Trionians and the businesspeople are obvious? What similarities are obvious?

411. THE GOLD WATCH: BALANCING PERSONAL AND PROFESSIONAL VALUES

Goals

I. To provide an opportunity for the participants to examine, identify, and clarify their personal and professional values.

II. To allow the participants to explore the interrelationship of personal values and values expressed by and in organizations.

Group Size

Three to five groups of four to six participants each.

Time Required

Two hours.

Materials

I. A copy of The Gold Watch Work Sheet for each participant.

II. A copy of The Gold Watch Discussion Sheet for each participant.

III. A pencil for each participant.

IV. A sheet of newsprint and a felt-tipped marker for each group.

V. Masking tape for each group.

VI. A clipboard or other portable writing surface for each group's recorder.

Physical Setting

A room large enough so that each group can work with a degree of privacy and without disturbing the other groups. Each group also should be placed near a wall so that a sheet of newsprint can be displayed within the view of all of its members.

Process

I. The facilitator introduces the goals of the activity.

II. The participants are assembled into groups of four to six each and are given copies of The Gold Watch Work Sheet and pencils.

III. The facilitator asks the participants to read the situation presented in the work sheet and to follow the instructions at the end of the handout. (Fifteen minutes.)

IV. The members of each group are instructed to share their rankings with one another, explaining their rationales and articulating their associated values and beliefs as clearly as possible. The facilitator emphasizes that no opinions are to be expressed regarding another member's decisions or beliefs; requests for clarification are the only permissible comments. (Fifteen minutes.)

V. Each group is given a sheet of newsprint, a felt-tipped marker, and masking tape. The members of each group are told to try to reach a consensus regarding the ranking of any or all of the characters. The facilitator stipulates that if the group achieves a consensus, one member should be appointed to post the sheet of newsprint and to record the group's decisions on this sheet; if no consensus is possible, nothing is to be posted. After clarifying the task as necessary, the facilitator instructs the participants to begin. (Twenty minutes.)

VI. The facilitator distributes copies of The Gold Watch Discussion Sheet and asks the members of each group to discuss answers to questions on the sheet. Each group is instructed to select a recorder to take notes about the group's answers and to share these notes later with the total group; the facilitator gives each group a clipboard or other portable writing surface for the recorder's use. (Thirty minutes.)

VII. The total group is reconvened, and the recorders are asked to take turns sharing their notes. (Fifteen minutes.)

VIII. The facilitator leads a discussion of possible applications of what has been learned. The following questions are asked:

1. Which of your attitudes or values have you questioned as a result of this experience? Which have been reaffirmed for you as a result of this experience?

2. What changes might you consider making in your own behavior in your organization? What is one action step that you might take toward such a change?

3. How could what you have learned be of help to your organization? What might you recommend or suggest to your organization?

Variations

I. During Step III the facilitator may stipulate that each participant not only follow the instructions on the work sheet but also write an ending to the situation presented. Subsequently, the members of each group compare their compositions.

II. During Step IV each participant may be asked to state which character in the story he or she would want to be and to explain how that would make a difference in the outcome.

III. After Step VI each group may be asked to write the story of the gold watch as it should have happened, based on the values that have been expressed in the group.

IV. Other value issues may be dealt with by changing the ranking instructions to reflect least/most responsible, least/most powerful, least/most caring, and so forth.

Similar Structured Experiences: *'81 Annual:* Structured Experience **283;** *'83 Annual:* **339;** *Vol. IX:* **362;** *'84 Annual:* **374, 375.**

Suggested Instrument: *'85 Annual,* p. 107: "The Personal Value Statement (PVS): An Experiential Learning Instrument."

Notes on the Use of "The Gold Watch":

Submitted by Michael R. Lavery. "The Gold Watch" was inspired by "Louisa's Problem" (*'81 Annual,* Structured Experience 283). The author would like to express his appreciation to his 3M Germany business students, who responded enthusiastically to this activity and suggested that it might be worthy of a wider audience.

THE GOLD WATCH WORK SHEET

Situation

Ringo is a thirty-five-year-old salesman with Anderson and Company, an old, established wholesaler of British office equipment. He lives near Anderson's headquarters in London with his wife and two adopted children.

On a recent sales tour of the Persian Gulf, Ringo met *Abdul,* an office-equipment supplier who was interested in a line of photocopiers worth £250,000. Abdul told Ringo that he would give Ringo an order for the photocopiers in return for a gold Rolex watch worth £7,000. Abdul showed Ringo the watch he wanted in a catalog, and Ringo said that he would see what he could do.

On returning to London, Ringo told *Charles,* his boss, about the proposition, asking if he could go ahead and buy the Rolex in order to obtain the order. Charles was outraged and said, "This is immoral! It's not decent British business practice to offer bribes. We're living in a civilized society. If I find out that you've been bribing customers to get orders, I'll fire you on the spot! Have I made myself clear?"

After the confrontation with Charles, Ringo left the office and drove to the home of *Angus,* his friend and colleague. He explained his plight and then said, "What can I do, Angus? It's an important order, and there's a chance of repeat business; Abdul is interested in office furniture and typewriters as well as additional photocopiers in the future."

Angus thought for a moment and then said, "Ringo, why don't you finance the deal yourself? Buy the bloody watch and land the contract. With your commission and any future business, you'll get a decent return on your investment. Don't even tell Charles; he's so bloody old-fashioned—he has no idea how to do business with our Arab friends."

Ringo left Angus's home, went to his car, thought for a few minutes, and then drove to his bank. *Mr. Grey,* the bank manager and a close friend of Ringo's father, listened to Ringo's reasons for wanting the loan of £7,000. Despite the fact that Ringo's checking account was overdrawn, he agreed to give Ringo the loan immediately.

The next day Ringo went to a jewelry store near his office and asked a clerk for the specific Rolex watch requested by Abdul. While he was waiting for the clerk to bring him the watch, *Jane,* Charles's secretary, came into the store to buy a birthday present for her mother. Unobserved by Ringo, she watched as the clerk gave the watch to Ringo in exchange for £7,000 cash. In her astonishment she forgot about finding a present for her mother, hurried back to Anderson and Company, burst into Charles's office, and asked, "How can a salesman who earns £13,000 a year afford a £7,000 watch?"

Charles was furious. He rushed out of his office and found Ringo just returning from the jewelry store. "You're fired!" he shouted.

"Let me explain...," muttered Ringo.

"No excuses! I warned you!"

At that moment a Telex came through; it read as follows: "NO LONGER INTERESTED IN PHOTOCOPIER DEAL. FOUND ALTERNATIVE SUP-PLIER. ABDUL."

Instructions

Rank order the following characters from *1* (least objectionable) to *6* (most objectionable):

_____ Ringo

_____ Abdul

_____ Charles

_____ Angus

_____ Mr. Grey

_____ Jane

THE GOLD WATCH DISCUSSION SHEET

1. What past experiences were brought to mind by the story of the gold watch? Which character did you identify with most strongly?

2. How were your rankings related to any differences between your personal and professional values? What choices did you have to make?

3. What similarities in rankings arose among the members of your group? What differences arose?

4. What issues seemed most important to your group?

5. How did value conflicts within your group affect the consensus process? How was conflict over values resolved?

6. What did this experience show you about the nature of individual values?

7. What can you generalize about an individual's personal and professional values? What can you infer about the congruence of personal values and values expressed by or in organizations?

8. What might be some ways to negotiate value conflicts in organizations?

412. CLIENT CONCERNS: DEVELOPING APPROPRIATE TRAINER RESPONSES

Goals

I. To develop the participants' skills in devising appropriate responses to representative client statements.

II. To offer the participants an opportunity to explore ways of handling various client concerns and expectations.

III. To help the participants to identify their individual biases about various training issues.

Group Size

Two to four groups of four or five trainers each.

Time Required

One hour and forty-five minutes.

Materials

I. A copy of the Client Concerns Work Sheet for each participant.

II. A pencil for each participant.

III. Blank paper for each group's reporter.

IV. A newsprint flip chart and a felt-tipped marker.

V. Masking tape for posting newsprint.

Physical Setting

A room large enough so that the individual groups can work without disturbing one another. Chairs and writing surfaces should be provided for the participants.

Process

I. The goals of the activity are explained.

II. Each participant is given a copy of the Client Concerns Work Sheet and a pencil and is asked to work independently to complete the sheet. (Twenty minutes.)

III. The participants are assembled into groups of four or five each, and each group is instructed to exchange its members' work sheets with those of another group. The facilitator clarifies that the participants need not write their names on their work sheets unless they wish to retrieve their sheets after the conclusion of the activity.

IV. The members of each group are instructed to review and discuss the responses received in the exchange and to select the best response for each client statement. Each group also is instructed to select one member who will record the group's choices, report these choices later to the total group, and explain the group members' rationale for choosing as they did; blank paper is given to each group so that the reporter may take notes. The facilitator further stipulates that if the group cannot achieve a consensus about the best response for a particular statement, the members should either alter one of the existing responses to improve it or devise a new response. (Forty-five minutes.)

V. After the groups have completed their work, the total group is reassembled. The reporters are instructed to share the group selections and the rationales for these selections. During this process the facilitator lists and posts the reported responses on newsprint. (Twenty minutes.)

VI. The facilitator leads a discussion of the activity by asking the following questions:

1. What personal reactions did you have to the client statements? Which of your reactions might be linked to your own personal biases about training? How did you deal with these biases in composing your responses?
2. What criteria did you use in composing your responses? What criteria did your group use in choosing the best responses? What patterns are evident in these criteria?
3. What can you conclude about ways of handling various client concerns? What are some "dos and don'ts" to keep in mind when dealing with client concerns? How can these "dos and don'ts" be translated into necessary trainer skills?
4. What will you do differently the next time you are confronted with a client statement similar to those on the work sheet? What new skills might you want to develop? How could you develop these skills?

Variations

I. After Step VI the participants may be asked to engage in action planning focused on skill acquisition.

II. After Step VI the participants may be asked to role play the situations represented by the client statements on the work sheet.

III. If the participants are all in-house trainers within a particular organization, the facilitator may rewrite the client statements on the work sheet to reflect that organization's training problems.

Lecturette Source: *'78 Annual*, p. 138: "Contracting: A Process and a Tool."

Notes on the Use of "Client Concerns":

CLIENT CONCERNS WORK SHEET

Instructions: Imagine that each of the following statements is made to you by a client. For each statement write a response and your rationale for this response.

Statement 1

"I think there's something going on in the production department of my company. I'd like you to run a communication-skills workshop as soon as you can for the people in this department."

Response

Rationale

Statement 2

"It's been six months since we had our supervisors go through that training program you conducted, and I don't see any changes. We've still got the same turnover problem."

Response

Rationale

Adapted from L. D. Goodstein, "Training Manager Interaction Test," University Associates, 1983.

Structured Experience 412

Statement 3

"It's extremely important that my people use what they've learned from the program you just conducted. What can I do to help?"

Response

Rationale

Statement 4

"How can I be sure that the training program you've outlined will really help solve the performance problems I'm having with my people?"

Response

Rationale

Statement 5

"I'd like to let you know how I feel about that leadership program you told us about. We hired the people you recommended to conduct it, and they weren't at all well received. They used a lot of abstract language and talked over the heads of most of our people!"

Response

Rationale

CONTRIBUTORS

B.J. Allen, Jr., Ed.D.
Associate Professor of Social Studies
  Education
Curriculum and Instruction
College of Education
Florida State University
Tallahassee, Florida 32306
(904) 644-6553

Joseph J. Blase, Ph.D.
Assistant Professor of Educational
  Administration
Department of Educational
  Administration
College of Education
University of Georgia
Athens, Georgia 30602
(404) 542-3343

Jane C. Bryant
5490 Plano Road
Bowling Green, Kentucky 42101
(502) 781-6148

Alan R. Carey
304 Clinton Court
Wheaton, Illinois 60187
(312) 682-4568

Carlo E. Cetti
Director of Management
  and Franchise Training
Foodmaker, Inc.
9330 Balboa Avenue
San Diego, California 92123
(619) 571-2121

S. Chintamani
Senior Faculty Member
State Bank Staff College
State Bank of India
6-3-1188, High Cliff, Begumpet
Hyderabad - 500016
India
37519

James I. Costigan, Ph.D.
Chair, Department of Communication
Fort Hays State University
600 Park Street
Hays, Kansas 67601-4099
(913) 628-5365

Mary Kirkpatrick Craig
Project Manager, Training Department
Foodmaker, Inc.
9330 Balboa Avenue
San Diego, California 92123
(619) 571-2121

Dale N. DeHaven
Job Orientation and Work Group
  Training Facilitator
General Motors-Pontiac Motor Division
Plant Engineering, Plant 8,
  Car Assembly
One Pontiac Plaza
Pontiac, Michigan 48053
(313) 857-4459

Patrick Doyle
Principal
High Impact Training Services
RR 2 Perth Road Village
Ontario K0H 2L0
Canada
(613) 353-6517

Alan Gilburg
President
The TEAMWORK Company
647 Lafayette Avenue
Buffalo, New York 14222-1439
(716) 882-1112

Michael L. Gracey
Vice President
c/o UAW Local 653
990 Joslyn Avenue
Pontiac, Michigan 48053
(313) 334-9917

Judith L. Grewell
Executive Assistant/Director of Training
Greenbriar Trust
7071 Orchard Lake Road, Suite 255
West Bloomfield, Michigan 48033
(313) 855-1160

Bunty Ketcham
Bunty Ketcham & Associates
Two East Melrose Street
Chevy Chase, Maryland 20815
(301) 654-0429

William B. Kline, Ph.D.
Assistant Professor of Counseling
Department of Educational
  Administration and Counseling
College of Education
University of Northern Iowa
508 Education Center
Cedar Falls, Iowa 50614
(319) 273-3362

Michael R. Lavery
Management Language Trainer
3M Germany Human Resources
  Development
Carl Schurz Strasse 1
4040 Neuss 1
West Germany
02101-142728

Linda Costigan Lederman, Ph.D.
Assistant Professor
  and Communication Consultant
Department of Communication
SCILS
Rutgers University
4 Huntington Street
New Brunswick, New Jersey 08903
(201) 932-8295

Edward F. Pajak, Ph.D.
Assistant Professor of Education
Department of Curriculum
  and Supervision
124 Aderhold Hall
College of Education
University of Georgia
Athens, Georgia 30602
(404) 542-1343

Thomas H. Patten, Jr., Ph.D.
Professor
Department of Management
  and Human Resources
School of Business Administration
California State Polytechnic University
3801 West Temple Avenue
Pomona, California 91768
(714) 598-0447

Geraldine Platt
Facilitator in G-Car Orientation
G-Car Training
General Motors-Pontiac Motor Division
One Pontiac Plaza
Pontiac, Michigan 48053
(313) 857-0939

Larry Porter, Ph.D.
Senior Consultant
University Associates, Inc.
8517 Production Avenue
San Diego, California 92121
(619) 578-5900

Gustave J. Rath, Ph.D.
Professor
Department of Industrial Engineering
  and Management Sciences
The Technological Institute
Northwestern University
Evanston, Illinois 60201-9990
(312) 491-3668

Lea P. Stewart, Ph.D.
Assistant Professor
Department of Communication/
  School of Communication,
  Information and Library Studies
Rutgers University
4 Huntington Street
New Brunswick, New Jersey 08903
(201) 932-8563

Gilles L. Talbot
Professor of Psychology
Champlain Regional College
St-Lawrence Campus
790, Neree Tremblay Street
Ste-Foy, Quebec G1V 4K2
Canada
(418) 656-6921. ext. 143

Sandra K. Tyson
Department of Biology
Fort Hays State University
600 Park Street
Hays, Kansas 67601-4099
(913) 628-4212

STRUCTURED EXPERIENCE CATEGORIES

Please add the following name to your mailing list.

UA

_____

_____

_____

_____ Zip _____

Primary Organizational Affiliation: [ ] fill in with one
number from below

1. Education
2. Business & Industry
3. Religious Organization
4. Government Agency
5. Counseling

6. Mental Health
7. Community, Voluntary, and/or
   Service Organization
8. Health Care
9. Library
0. Consulting

Please add the following name to your mailing list.

UA

_____

_____

_____

_____ Zip _____

Primary Organizational Affiliation: [ ] fill in with one
number from below

1. Education
2. Business & Industry
3. Religious Organization
4. Government Agency
5. Counseling

6. Mental Health
7. Community, Voluntary, and/or
   Service Organization
8. Health Care
9. Library
0. Consulting

BUSINESS REPLY CARD

FIRST CLASS   PERMIT NO. 11201 SAN DIEGO, CA

POSTAGE WILL BE PAID BY ADDRESSEE

UNIVERSITY ASSOCIATES
Publishers and Consultants
8517 Production Avenue
P.O. Box 26240
San Diego, California 92126

NO POSTAGE
NECESSARY
IF MAILED
IN THE
UNITED STATES

BUSINESS REPLY CARD

FIRST CLASS   PERMIT NO. 11201 SAN DIEGO, CA

POSTAGE WILL BE PAID BY ADDRESSEE

UNIVERSITY ASSOCIATES
Publishers and Consultants
8517 Production Avenue
P.O. Box 26240
San Diego, California 92126